Christianity in Modern China

Series Editor
Cindy Yik-yi Chu, Department of History, Hong Kong Baptist
University, Kowloon Tong, Hong Kong

This series addresses Christianity in China from the time of the late Ming and early Qing dynasties to the present. It includes a number of disciplines—history, political science, theology, religious studies, gender studies and sociology. Not only is the series inter-disciplinary, it also encourages inter-religious dialogue. It covers the presence of the Catholic Church, the Protestant Churches and the Orthodox Church in China. While Chinese Protestant Churches have attracted much scholarly and journalistic attention, there is much unknown about the Catholic Church and the Orthodox Church in China. There is an enormous demand for monographs on the Chinese Catholic Church and the Orthodox Church. This series captures the breathtaking phenomenon of the rapid expansion of Chinese Christianity on the one hand, and the long awaited need to reveal the reality and the development of Chinese Catholicism and the Orthodox religion on the other.

Christianity in China reflects on the tremendous importance of Chinese-foreign relations. The series touches on many levels of research—the life of a single Christian in a village, a city parish, the conflicts between converts in a province, the policy of the provincial authority and state-to-state relations. It concerns the influence of different cultures on Chinese soil—the American, the French, the Italian, the Portuguese and so on. Contributors of the series include not only people from the academia but journalists and professional writers as well. The series would stand out as a collective effort of authors from different countries and backgrounds. Under the influence of globalization, it is entirely necessary to emphasize the intercultural dimension of the monographs of the series. With Christianity being questioned in the Western world, as witnessed in the popularity of Dan Brown's books since some time ago, the Chinese have surprised the world by their embracement of this foreign religion.

NOW INDEXED ON SCOPUS!

More information about this series at
https://link.springer.com/bookseries/14895

Cindy Yik-yi Chu
Editor

The Catholic Church,
The Bible,
and Evangelization
in China

palgrave
macmillan

Editor
Cindy Yik-yi Chu
Department of History
Hong Kong Baptist University
Hong Kong

ISSN 2730-7875   ISSN 2730-7883   (electronic)
Christianity in Modern China
ISBN 978-981-16-6184-6   ISBN 978-981-16-6182-2   (eBook)
https://doi.org/10.1007/978-981-16-6182-2

Cover illustration: © Melisa Hasan

This Palgrave Macmillan imprint is published by the registered company Springer Nature Singapore Pte Ltd.
The registered company address is: 152 Beach Road, #21-01/04 Gateway East, Singapore 189721, Singapore

To Sister Betty Ann Maheu, MM

PREFACE

Many approaches and perspectives have been adopted in the study of the Catholic Church in China. The Church's vibrant history is explored in this collection of articles, with topics including politics, the establishment of the Church, evangelization through service and the Bible, and the day-to-day running of local churches, with examples of the Jiangnan region (an area south of the Yangtze River including large cities such as Shanghai, Nanjing, and Ningbo) and the recollections of a Chinese convert. The authors contribute insights into the many layers of the Chinese Catholic Church, addressing the relations between the state and the Church, cross-cultural relations between foreign missionaries and local people, and the concerted effort to spread the Good News throughout society. It is only by acknowledging the complexity of the Church that we can do justice to the people who have contributed to the Christian faith in China.

The history of the Chinese Catholic Church is complex and multi-layered. This complexity is reflected in the heated debates about Beijing's agreement with the Vatican on the appointment of bishops. On September 22, 2018, the Holy See and China signed a historic provisional agreement stating that Pope Francis can appoint bishops recommended by Beijing, resolving the decades-long problem of the consecration of Chinese bishops that had not received the Pope's approval.[1] Subsequently, the Pope approved seven bishops nominated by Beijing. Pope Francis expressed the hope that "the wounds of the past" would be healed and that there would be "the full communion of all Chinese Catholics."[2]

In 2020, the Holy See and China agreed to renew the agreement until October 22, 2022.[3]

This collection of articles begins with the perspectives of Beijing on the role of religion in serving state interests. From the Chinese Communists' point of view, unless religion acts as a stabilizing force in society, Christian churches will lose their reason to exist. This might be incomprehensible to Western Christians, who value freedom of religion and their right to practice their faith. In China, however, Christians have "freedom of religious belief," meaning that they can only practice their faith in designated places of worship. The Beijing government claims that Chinese Catholics cannot be loyal to the Pope, who is seen as a foreign authority that threatens the government's power. While Beijing emphasizes the duty of Chinese Christians to work toward the country's modernization, Catholics abroad prioritize their right to religious expression. The source of conflict between Beijing and the underground Church in China, together with foreign observers, has been the debate surrounding the use of religion to serve state interests and the freedom to choose one's religion without political interference. Since the 1980s, China has established several government organizations to monitor the activities of Catholics, including the Chinese Catholic Patriotic Association (CCPA), the Bishops' Conference of the Catholic Church in China, and Chinese Catholic Church Administrative Commission.

Another key topic area in the study of the Chinese Catholic Church is gender. The study of the Chinese Catholic Church began with assessments of the service activities of foreign missionaries and societies, including relief efforts, education, and health care. Scholars have gradually given more attention to the history of Chinese converts to Catholicism, who were the recipients of these missionaries' service. There has been an emphasis on understanding both foreigners and Chinese in the Catholic Church, and this cross-cultural exchange places foreign missionaries and Chinese converts on equal footing in academic works. The Italian Canossian Sisters arrived in Hong Kong in 1860, shortly before the Beijing Convention, which was implemented in response to the Second Opium War (1856–1860). After foreign priests had established their mission fields, non-Chinese Catholic nuns served Chinese women and children by opening schools and hospitals and providing social services and welfare. While the study of foreign nuns in China compensates to some degree for the lack of scholarly work on women in the Chinese Catholic Church, there are very few works on Chinese nuns and female converts. It is impossible to offset the imbalance in the study of Chinese men and women in the Catholic Church because of the lack of research materials available for the study of women. This gap is likely due to high illiteracy levels in the villages where much of the missionaries' work took place.

Researchers continue to venture into unknown areas to explore the many manifestations of cross-cultural exchange. The translation of the Bible into Chinese was a great step forward in the evangelization and localization of the Catholic Church in China. Italian Franciscan Father Gabriele Allegra (1907–1976) established the Studium Biblicum Franciscanum Sinense (or Sigao Shengjing Xuehui/Scotus Bible Association, which relocated from Beijing to Hong Kong in 1948), which published a fully translated Bible in 1968. This Chinese version of the Bible, known as the Studium Biblicum Version (*Sigao Shengjing*), is still used in Hong Kong today. In mainland China, however, Chinese Catholics only gained access to the Studium Biblicum Version (*Sigao Shengjing*) much later, in 1992. The spread of knowledge has been slower among Catholics in mainland China than among those living in other areas, underscoring the differences in levels of understanding of the Catholic doctrine between various societal groups in Chinese society. The study of the acceptance of the various versions of the Bible in contemporary China highlights behavioral changes among people of different age groups and demographic backgrounds in Chinese society.

The Chinese Catholic Church has endured a variety of political and social movements under Communist rule in China since the 1950s. The Anti-Rightist Movement of 1957 targeted Catholics in the Jiangnan region. The Beijing government's Religious Affairs Bureau established the Chinese Catholic Patriotic Association (CCPA) in 1957, whose objectives were to regulate and control the activities of the Catholic population. Bishop Ignatius Gong Pinmei of Shanghai, along with other prominent Catholics, opposed the Communist regime, but his resistance quickly failed and he was later imprisoned. The Communist Party's United Front strategy of uniting its supporters and rallying neutral citizens against its enemies has been the guiding principle for handling the Chinese Catholics. This strategy was especially prevalent when China opened to the world in 1979, and the existence of the Open Church and the Underground Church raised questions among the various government authorities regarding the cultivation of a Catholic identity, with Beijing forcing Catholics to question their loyalty to their country and to the Pope.

This collection of articles represents the concerted efforts of Chinese, Italian, and American scholars living in China, Europe, and the United States and who belong to various disciplines, such as History, Religious Studies, and Language Studies, to promote a better understanding of the Catholic Church in China and throughout the world.

NOTE ON NAMES OF PEOPLE AND PLACES

Pinyin is used for the names of people and places in China mainland, for example Xi Jinping and Sheshan, respectively. As for Chinese Catholics on the mainland, their Christian names appear before their Chinese names, for example Aloysius Jin Luxian—Jin being his family name and Luxian being the combination of the two Chinese characters that follow his family name. Another example is Ignatius Gong Pinmei—Gong being his family name and Pinmei being the two Chinese characters that follow his family name.

Kowloon, Hong Kong   Cindy Yik-yi Chu

NOTES

1. "Vatican and China Sign Agreement on Bishop Appointments," *The Guardian*, September 22, 2018, https://www.theguardian.com/world/2018/sep/22/vatican-and-china-sign-agreement-on-bishop-appointments (Accessed January 13, 2021); "Communiqué concerning the signing of a Provisional Agreement between the Holy See and the People's Republic of China on the appointment of Bishops, 22.09.2018," September 22, 2018, https://press.vatican.va/content/salastampa/en/bollettino/pubblico/2018/09/22/180922d.html (Accessed January 13, 2021).
2. "Vatican Announces Deal with China on Bishop Appointments," *NBC News*, September 22, 2018, https://www.nbcnews.com/news/world/vatican-announces-deal-china-bishop-appointments-n912186 (Accessed January 13, 2021).
3. "Holy See and China Renew Provisional Agreement for 2 Years," *Vatican News*, October 22, 2020, https://www.vaticannews.va/en/vatican-city/news/2020-10/holy-see-china-provisional-agreement-renew-appointment-bishops.html (Accessed January 13, 2021).

CONTENTS

Notes on Contributors

Cindy Yik-yi Chu is Professor of History at Hong Kong Baptist University. She writes on the Catholic Church and the Catholic sisters in China Mainland and Hong Kong. She has published 16 books and 50 some articles in edited volumes and journals. Her works include: Edited with Paul P. Mariani, *People, Communities, and the Catholic Church in China* (Singapore: Palgrave Pivot, 2020), *The Chinese Sisters of the Precious Blood and the Evolution of the Catholic Church* (Palgrave, 2016), and *Catholicism in China, 1900–Present* (Editor, Palgrave, 2014). She is interested in the history of the Catholic Church in modern and contemporary China and Hong Kong, Catholic sisters in Chinese societies, and Sino–Vatican relations. She is now editing *The Palgrave Handbook of the Catholic Church in East Asia* and working on the history of Sino–Vatican relations.

Gianni Criveller was born in Treviso (Italy) and is a missionary and priest with PIME (Pontifical Institute for Foreign Missions). He is Dean of Studies and Professor of Theology at PIME International Missionary

School of Theology in Monza (Italy) and Advisor to the National Council of the Italian Theological Association. He is a theologian specializing in Christology, Theology of Mission, and the encounter between China and Christianity. He also teaches at the Holy Spirit Seminary College in Hong Kong and is a Research Fellow at the Chinese University of Hong Kong. He is a frequent speaker in academic symposiums around the world, especially on Jesuit missionaries to China (Matteo Ricci and Giulio Aleni), late Ming and early Qing Catholic missions, and the Chinese Rites Controversy. He has published about 20 books and hundreds of essays in specialized journals in various languages.

Raissa De Gruttola is Adjunct Professor of Chinese Language at Perugia University (Italy). She holds a Ph.D. in Asian and African Studies (Chinese) in the Department of Asian and North African Studies of the Ca' Foscari University of Venice (2017). Her Ph.D. dissertation is on Gabriele Allegra and the first complete translation of the Catholic Bible in Chinese. Among her publications are "The Studium Biblicum Franciscanum Sinense from 1976 to Present" in *People, Communities, and the Catholic Church in China*, edited by Cindy Yik-yi Chu and Paul P. Mariani (2020); "The Union Version and the Sigao Bible" in *Journal of the Royal Asiatic Society* (2020); "Translating the Bible into Chinese: Characteristics and Features of the Sigao Shengjing" in *Between Texts, Beyond Words: Intertextuality and Translation*, edited by Nicoletta Pesaro (2018).

Sheng-mei Ma is Professor of English at Michigan State University in Michigan, USA, specializing in Asian Diaspora and East-West comparative studies. He is the author of 10 books: *On East-West* (2021); *Off-White* (2019); *Sinophone-Anglophone Cultural Duet* (2017); *The Last Isle* (2015); *Alienglish* (2014); *Asian Diaspora and East-West Modernity* (2012); *Diaspora Literature and Visual Culture* (2011); *East-West Montage* (2007); *The Deathly Embrace* (2000); and *Immigrant Subjectivities in Asian American and Asian Diaspora Literatures* (1998). He is the co-editor of 4 books, including *Transnational Narratives in Englishes of Exile* (2018), and the author of a critical memoir *Immigrant Horse's Mouth: Journey to the West by Bearing East* (2022) as well as a collection of poetry in Chinese.

Steven Pieragastini is Lecturer in History at Whittier College. He received his Ph.D. in History from Brandeis University in 2017.

One of his publications is "A French University in China? The Forgotten History of Zhendan University (L'Université l'Aurore, 震旦大學 Zhendan daxue)," *Outre-Mers, Revue d'histoire* (2017). His book-in-progress focuses on the history of the Catholic Church in modern China and its relationship with the Chinese state.

Monica Romano is a sinologist holding a Ph.D. in Ethnology and Ethno-Anthropology from Sapienza University of Rome. She also studied in Beijing Language and Culture University and Fu Jen Catholic University in Taipei, and subsequently visited China Mainland and Hong Kong many times for her research. She is interested in Christianity in China, particularly the Catholic Church and Chinese Bible translation. She participated in several conferences in Italy and abroad. From 2013 to 2020, she was Lecturer at Pontifical Gregorian University in Rome, initially in the Faculty of Missiology and later in the Center of Interreligious Studies and the Faculty of Social Sciences. Her courses focused on Chinese Thought in Comparison with Christianity; Early Confucianism, Daoism, and Chinese Buddhism; Chinese Bible Translation; and the role of faith-based institutions in reducing poverty and promoting integral development.

Rachel Zhu Xiaohong is Associate Professor of Religious Studies at Fudan University, Shanghai. She specializes in Methodology of Religious Studies, Feminist Theology, Contemporary Catholic Philosophy and Theology, and Contemporary Roman Catholic Church in China. She was Visiting Scholar at Chinese Catholic Studies Initiatives, Saint John's University, Collegeville, Minnesota. She has published over 70 articles in journals and has co-written 3 books, translated 4, and coedited a further 4. She actively serves the local diocese and has been the Board Member of the Catholic Intelligentsia Association in Shanghai. She has also been a member of the Academic Committee for the Series of Systematic Theology in Brill Publishing House and Editorial Committee for the journal *Christian Thought Review*, China.

LIST OF FIGURES

LIST OF TABLES

PART I

The Catholic Church

CHAPTER 1

The Catholic Church in China in the 1980s: Identity, Loyalty, and Obedience

Cindy Yik-yi Chu

Abstract Religion in China is expected to stabilize and harmonize society. Beijing has not wanted to see Chinese Christians being outspoken in their faith and activities. This chapter addresses the conflicts between the Vatican and Beijing in the 1980s. After China opened to the world in 1979, the people could practice their religion in public as Beijing experimented with its policy toward religion. Yet while the decade began with optimism for greater cooperation between Rome and Beijing, it ended with the CCP's open condemnation of the Vatican and the Pope. From Beijing's perspective, the core problem that was aroused in the 1980s was who should control the Chinese Catholics, the Vatican or itself. This issue necessarily involved the identity, loyalty, and obedience of the Chinese Catholics.

C. Y. Chu (✉)
Department of History, Hong Kong Baptist University, Hong Kong
e-mail: cindychu@hkbu.edu.hk

C. Y. Chu (ed.), *The Catholic Church, The Bible, and Evangelization in China*, Christianity in Modern China,
https://doi.org/10.1007/978-981-16-6182-2_1

Keywords Sino–Vatican relations · Chinese Catholic Patriotic Association · United front · The Vatican · Beijing · Ignatius Gong Pinmei · Aloysius Jin Luxian · Dominic Deng Yiming

As in other Communist states, such as Cuba and Laos,[1] religion in China is expected to be a stabilizing and harmonizing force in society.[2] Given this expectation, the Beijing government has traditionally encouraged Chinese Christians to avoid practicing their faith in an outspoken manner. In the December 2001 National Religious Work Meeting, which was co-organized by the State Council and the Politburo (indicating the link between the government and the Chinese Communist Party), the General Secretary of the Chinese Communist Party (CCP), Jiang Zemin (江泽民, born 1926), who was greatly concerned with China's stability, stated that religion could be used as a stabilizing force in society and have a positive effect on the country's development.[3]

This chapter discusses the conflicts between the Vatican and Beijing in the 1980s. After China opened to the world in 1979, Beijing experimented with a more relaxed policy toward religion, allowing its citizens to practice their respective faiths in public. Yet although the decade began with optimism for greater cooperation between the Vatican and Beijing, it ended with the CCP's open condemnation of the Catholic Church and the Pope. Beijing, looking to exercise control over its people, denounced the Vatican's attempts to exert increasing influence over China's Catholic community.

This issue necessarily involved questions of identity, loyalty, and obedience for Chinese Catholics. Beginning in the 1980s, Chinese Christian intellectuals were faced with the pressing question: "who am I?"[4] Like all Christians in China, Chinese Catholics had a dual Chinese–Christian identity, of which Beijing was suspicious. The title of John Peale's book *The Love of God in China: Can One Be Both Chinese and Christian?*[5] highlights this identity issue. Chinese Catholics were caught in the middle of the Sino–Vatican conflict, and they struggled with their loyalty to the state and their commitment to their faith.

Beijing believed that Western countries used Christianity to subvert power in China.[6] When trouble arose, Beijing adopted stringent policies toward Chinese Catholics and demanded absolute obedience. The determination to prevent outside participation and interference in China's internal affairs has been a defining characteristic of China's modern history since the second half of the nineteenth century, when the country was under foreign rule. On the issue of the Vatican's outward support of the recognition of Taiwan's independence, for instance, Beijing has repeatedly stated that the Vatican should not use religious matters as an excuse to interfere in China's domestic politics.[7]

In the 1980s, the Beijing government looked to exercise greater control over the Chinese Catholic Church, with an eye toward creating a national Church under its complete control.[8] This situation further deepened the identity crisis of Chinese Catholics, who looked to the overseas authority of the Pope to guide their faith but were obliged to demonstrate allegiance to the ruling Communist authorities. Article 36 of the Constitution of the People's Republic of China (PRC), adopted in 1982, provides for freedom of religious belief and the right to organize religious activities, but with two caveats: religious beliefs can only be expressed in places designated for worship, and religion must not have an adverse effect on the social order. Furthermore, religious bodies (such as the Chinese Catholic Church) cannot be subject to external authority. Against the backdrop of the complex relationship between religion and politics in Communist China, Beijing continues to enforce these policies. As Article 36 states[9]:

> Citizens of the People's Republic of China enjoy freedom of religious belief.
> No state organ, public organization or individual may compel citizens to believe in, or
> not to believe in, any religion; nor may they discriminate against citizens who believe
> in, or do not believe in, any religion.
> The state protects normal religious activities. No one may make use of religion to
> engage in activities that disrupt public order, impair the health of citizens or interfere with the educational system of the state.
> Religious bodies and religious affairs must not be subject to any foreign control.

As a result of the Communist Party's policy on religion, two communities formed within the Chinese Catholic Church: the Open Church (official, registered, state-controlled) and the Underground Church (unofficial, unregistered, refusing state control). In spite of the existence of these two communities, the Chinese Catholic Church has remained united, an idea which has been rejected by both the Vatican and the Beijing government. In the 1980s, the Chinese Catholic Patriotic Association (CCPA 中国天主教爱国会), the Bishops' Conference of the Catholic Church in China (中国天主教主教团), and the Chinese Catholic Church Administrative Commission (中国天主教教务委员会) were the institutions most visibly in charge of the Open Church in China.

Chinese Catholics are expected to demonstrate absolute patriotism to the Chinese state, and the notion of dual Chinese Christian identity is unacceptable to the Beijing government. Loyalty to the Vatican is interpreted as denial of the authority of the state, as represented by both the government and the CCP. In the 1980s, the threat of foreign interference in China's internal affairs continued to trouble authorities at the national level, who feared the Vatican's influence on the activities of both the high-level clergy and on Chinese Catholics.

EARLY COMMUNIST POLICIES TOWARD CHRISTIANS

In 1950, "A group of celebrities led by representatives of the National Council of the Chinese Young People's Christian Association released a declaration calling on the Christians to cut off their links with the imperialist powers."[10] In 1951, Wu Yaozong (吴耀宗, 1893–1979), together with the Communist authorities, founded the Three-Self Patriotic Movement for Chinese Protestants (三自爱国运动, or 三自教会). Implemented on an enormous scale across China, the movement promoted the independence of the Chinese Protestant Church from foreign influence. The movement's three basic tenets, self-government, self-support, and self-propagation (自治, 自养, 自传[11]), were developed in discussions between Premier Zhou Enlai and influential Chinese Christians under the leadership of Wu Yaozong.[12] While the Three-Self Patriotic Movement allowed Beijing to exert control over Chinese Protestants, it also demanded obedience from Chinese Catholics. The movement's objectives were to eliminate foreign interference in the Chinese Christian Churches, thereby ensuring the complete loyalty of Chinese Christians to the state and the CCP while simultaneously allowing these individuals to preserve their Christian identity.[13]

In 1954, the Religious Affairs Department became the Bureau of Religious Affairs, which reported directly to the State Council. At that time,

Shanghai was the center of Catholic opposition to government interference, where Bishop Ignatius Gong Pinmei led the resistance movement against political control over religion. In 1955, the Shanghai authorities arrested Gong, who refused to denounce the Pope. In the same year, approximately 1,500 Chinese Catholics, including priests, Church leaders, and nuns, were imprisoned in Shanghai.[14] The government also mounted fierce attacks on Bishop Dominic Deng Yiming, S.J. (邓以明主教, 1908–1995) and Catholics in Guangzhou.[15]

CHINA'S OPENING TO THE WORLD

In December 1978, China embarked on its Four Modernizations plan under the direction of Deng Xiaoping (邓小平, 1904–1997), who warned that the mistakes of the Cultural Revolution (1966–1976) should never be repeated. Rather than mass movements like those that had taken place from 1949 to 1976, Deng emphasized that China should engage in agricultural reform, industrialization, the development of advanced scientific and technological knowledge, and military reconstruction. During the Cultural Revolution, all churches were closed.[16] With China's goal of opening to the world, the churches gradually reopened. This reopening, however, reignited concerns over whether Beijing and the Vatican could engage in a constructive dialogue. The Vatican made the mistakes of failing to keep China informed, acting too fast, and not recognizing the feelings of the Chinese side.[17]

Confounding this problem was the coexistence of the Open Church and the Underground Church in China. Members of the Open Church accepted the leadership of the CCPA (see below) and adhered to the policies of the Beijing government. The Open Church sought to cultivate patriotism among Catholics by stipulating that its priests were government-approved and monitored by the political authority of the CCPA. Underground Catholics, however, continued to conduct religious services in unregistered churches and insisted that the official regulations pertaining to religious expression had no meaning for them.

BEIJING'S CONTROL OVER
THE OPEN CHURCH SINCE 1979

In 1979, the State Council reinstated the Bureau of Religious Affairs, which had been shut down in 1975. In 1979, Beijing restored the

Three-Self Patriotic Movement, with two main tenets: Chinese Protestants should be loyal to the nation and Chinese Churches should be independent and free of foreign interference.[18]

The CCPA, the Bishops' Conference of the Catholic Church in China, and the Chinese Catholic Church Administrative Commission took an active role in the control of the Open Church. In June 1980, Beijing established the Bishops' Conference of the Catholic Church in China and the Chinese Catholic Church Administrative Commission.[19] While the former dealt with doctrinal problems,[20] the latter handled pastoral issues. The two organizations were thus responsible for internal matters in the Open Church.[21] The Bishops' Conference of the Catholic Church in China attempted to build close connections between the Chinese Church and the government.[22] As the conference became more prestigious in the 1980s, the CCPA allowed Catholics to participate in religious activities observed by government representatives, although exclusively in authorized churches.[23]

The Chinese Catholic Church has been characterized by conflict since 1979. Although Beijing has consistently emphasized the independence of the Chinese Church, in practice, this has meant independence from the religious and spiritual directives of the Pope. As Zhu aptly points out, "The Constitution of the CCPA clearly states that the Chinese Catholic Church must be independent and self-managed, which meant that it was to be completely cut off from the Vatican, both politically and financially, and later religiously."[24] However, China's Open Church has never been fully independent of the Beijing government. For example, in 1979, the Open Church was strictly controlled by the state and managed by the CCPA.[25] The consecration of more than 20 bishops between 1957 and 1980 without the consent of the Pope (see below) provided clear evidence that the CCPA and the Open Church functioned as a united entity under the Beijing government. In contrast to the Open Church, the Underground Church sought autonomy and rejected official leadership. In 1979, Catholic converts could still be found in China after the self-imposed isolation of Catholics in the late 1970s. The perpetuation of the Christian faith in China at that time depended solely on Chinese Catholics themselves.

THE BEGINNING OF SINO–VATICAN RELATIONS IN THE 1980S

The normalization of Sino–Vatican relations was complex. In August 1979, Pope John Paul II (1920–2005, r. 1978–2005) responded to China's interest in reconciling with foreign governments. In 1949, there were more than 3 million Chinese Catholics and around 100 bishops, 40 of whom were Chinese, and approximately 2,700 of China's roughly 5,800 Catholic priests were Chinese. Citing these striking figures, the Pope expressed his desire to reconnect with China's Catholic clergy and laity.[26] The Pope called the Chinese Catholic Church in 1949 "a living Church" in "perfect union with the Apostolic See."[27] Witnessing China's opening in 1979, the Pope hoped to engage directly with Chinese Catholics in the future and that religious freedom would become a reality in China.

The Pope's confidence was likely inspired by an event earlier that year in which more than 800 Catholics, Protestants, government representatives, and Communist cadres convened a conference in Shanghai.[28] Speakers at the conference condemned the Cultural Revolution and all false accusations against religion.[29] Beijing was clearly eager to demonstrate its seemingly positive attitude toward religion to the outside world. To this end, the government planned to reinstate the Bureau of Religious Affairs, which began operating two months later. In April 1979, the six Catholic churches in Beijing, Tianjin, Shanghai, Wuhan, Taiyuan, and Guangzhou reopened.

The United Front Work Department formulated the CCP's religious policy, seeking to "mobilize all positive elements, unify all possible strengths, and change negative elements to positive ones."[30] In Hong Kong, Bishop John Tong (汤汉主教, born 1939) commented that the relationship between religion and politics was the result of the Communists' united front strategy.[31] At the core of this strategy was "seeking unity" while striving to "preserve differences" among the people (*qiutong quanyi*).[32] The Communists aimed to rally supporters, including nonreligious citizens, with the goal of isolating and thus wining over their opponents, an approach with historical precedents in the prerevolutionary era.[33] Beijing constructed its religious policy as well as other policies on the basis of this strategy. According to Tong, the Bureau of Religious Affairs supported Beijing's efforts to form a united front as it coordinated, and administered the Four Modernizations program.

After the Pope's open request to establish relations with the Chinese Catholic Church, the Vatican sent its first senior official to China in late 1979. Soon after this request was made, Michael Fu Tieshan (傅铁山主教, 1931–2007) became the first Chinese bishop to be consecrated since China opened to the outside world. The principal consecrator and the two co-consecrators were bishops of the CCPA, and, crucially, the consecration was undertaken without Vatican involvement or approval. However, although the Vatican did not condone these actions, it remained eager to explore opportunities to work with Beijing. This eagerness could also be explained by China's decision that year to release many priests from prisons and work camps.

This period featured further official changes for the Chinese Catholic Church. Religious representatives from China confirmed the country's respect for basic religious freedoms in international conferences, and Chinese and Vatican representatives met for the first time since China's opening to the world. While the Vatican expressed concerns regarding the issue of the unsanctioned consecrations, political and religious leaders maintained a productive dialogue.

In spite of the tangible progress in Sino–Vatican relations, a 1979 Chinese law introduced new limits on religious expression, with the Fifth National People's Congress taking religious affairs under its control. Article 147 of the Criminal Law Code of 1979 stated that any deprivation of freedom of religious belief by state functionaries would lead to the detention or imprisonment of the perpetrators. While the law appeared to protect believers, it only protected what the state deemed to be "normal religious activities." "Abnormal religious activities" were defined very broadly and included any activities that were conducted in "an excessively frequent and long manner."[34] Through legal restrictions such as Article 147, the Beijing government controlled the Church's influence and placed greater legal pressures on the Underground Church.

In the early 1980s, while exploring ways in which to develop friendly relations with Beijing, Pope John Paul II expressed his conviction that Chinese Catholics could be faithfully Christian and patriotically Chinese at the same time.[35] In January 1982, the Pope sent a letter in which he expressed his hope that the Chinese Catholic Church would become part of the universal Church, and he included a call to Catholic bishops around the world to pray for the Church in China. In his letter, the Pope emphasized that the status of China's Church contributed to the unity of global Catholicism and had always been a special concern for him.[36]

China's Open Church reacted angrily to this letter, which it saw as an intrusion by the Vatican. The Beijing government found the letter equally alarming, as it interpreted the Pope's statement as a demand from the Vatican to interfere in China's internal affairs. According to Beijing, the Church should belong to the Chinese people without interference from the outside. The letter therefore acted as an obstacle to the improvement of the Vatican's diplomatic relationship with Beijing.

In response to Beijing's decision to consecrate Catholic bishops, the Vatican appointed its own bishops in China, a move condemned by Beijing. In 1981, the Vatican named Dominic Deng Yiming, S.J. (邓以明总主教), who was abroad at the time, Archbishop of Guangzhou, a decision that the CCPA vehemently opposed. Deng was the first bishop to declare his loyalty to the Vatican and to leave China. He was released from prison in June 1980 and arrived in Hong Kong several months later. When Deng returned to Hong Kong, Beijing attacked the Vatican for interfering in China's internal affairs and accused Deng of betraying his country.[37] Although the Pope appointed Catholic bishops elsewhere in the world, Beijing was fervently opposed to this happening in China, as the Vatican's interference in the Chinese Catholic Church represented the assertion of foreign authority in internal matters.

As a result, Beijing enacted laws to diminish the Vatican's influence in China. Hongyi Lai notes that "Document 19 in 1982 contained clauses that legalize sanction against the underground Catholic Church. It required religion to be self-reliant and independent of foreign influence and prohibited any foreign religious group from conducting missionary work in China."[38] The early 1980s were therefore characterized by Beijing's greater recourse to legal interventions against the Vatican and the Underground Church in China, with missionary work and unsanctioned religious services in particular being targets. In spite of the myriad of potential sources of conflict between the two sides, it was the issue of the unsanctioned consecrations of bishops that would have the most profound impact on Sino–Vatican relations through the remainder of the decade (see, for example, the case of Bishop Aloysius Jin Luxian (金鲁贤主教, 1916–2013), an important but controversial figure in the Chinese Church).[39]

THE STATE AND RELIGION

China's opening up brought changes to both the Open Church and the Underground Church. In the 1980s, the CCP and the government held supreme power over the Chinese state. The State Council of the government controlled the Bureau of Religious Affairs, while the Central Committee of the CCP was in charge of the United Front Work Department. The Bureau of Religious Affairs and the United Front Work Department jointly supervised the CCPA, which managed the clergy and the laity of the Open Church. In other words, the CCPA was the link between the state and the Church. The Open Church was therefore accountable to both the Bureau of Religious Affairs and the United Front Work Department.

The Open Church was subject to strict government control, although the organization was permitted to elect and consecrate its own bishops. It upheld the core ethos of the Three-Self Patriotic Movement, committing to freedom from foreign influence. As Charbonnier notes, by the mid-1980s, the Bishops' Conference of the Catholic Church in China had not made any meaningful moves nor engaged in conversations with other Asian bishops.[40] The Chinese Catholic Church Administrative Commission was more active in practical matters such as religious publications (e.g., the Bible, prayer books, catechism materials, and hymnals).[41] Cooperating with the CCPA, the Commission published an official periodical known as *Zhongguo Tianzhujiao* (The Catholic Church in China).[42] At the same time, the Open Church expressed the desire to offer pastoral services and sacraments and to provide Chinese Catholics with the opportunity to attend Mass.

Unlike the Open Church, the Underground Church did not have Beijing's approval and exclusively followed the teachings of the Vatican.[43] Nonetheless, the Underground Church amassed a strong following at the local level. Crucially, the Underground Church was unable to operate in an official capacity because its members were highly skeptical of government policies that contradicted their staunchly held religious and moral principles.

The CCP's policy on religion was documented by the Central Committee in March 1982 in a document entitled "The Basic Viewpoint and Policy on the Religious Question During Our Country's Socialist Period."[44] It outlined Beijing's interpretation of freedom of religious belief as follows: (1) "The main purpose of the policy of religious freedom is to unite believers and non-believers behind the task of reconstructing the nation"; (2) "Special care must be taken to prevent foreign religious organizations from infiltrating China"; and (3) "friendly relations with religious organizations abroad based on the principle of equality and mutual non-interference should be developed."[45]

The growing differences between China's Open Church and the Vatican also made it difficult for the former to accept the position of the latter for several reasons. First, although the Chinese people were becoming progressively better educated, the Open Church did not evolve sufficiently to reflect this major societal shift. For example, the Open Church was unable to fully comprehend the changes that resulted from the Second Vatican Council (1962–1965),[46] thereby isolating itself from other branches of the Catholic Church elsewhere in the world. Second, the Beijing government and the CCPA maintained total control over religious ceremonies, and ignored contemporary developments in global Catholicism introduced by the Pope. Third, the Open Church stood by China's one-child policy and the promotion of birth control, in staunch opposition to the Vatican's stance on procreation. Fourth, the Open Church followed Beijing in denouncing the Vatican's diplomatic ties with Taiwan.[47]

In spite of these many political differences and sources of potential conflict between Beijing and the Open Church, the 1980s saw a degree of freedom of religious belief that was unprecedented in the history of Communist China.[48] By July 1980, 33 bishops had been appointed by the government. China News Agency announced that in 1981 alone, a further dozen bishops had been consecrated without the Vatican's approval. By early 1982, China News Agency announced that more than 200 churches had been renovated for public use.[49]

By the mid-1980s, Catholic priests were preaching openly across the country and many cities had reopened their local churches. This was partly because they now belonged to the Open Church, which adhered to government directives. The CCPA worked with the Bureau of Religious Affairs to provide government grants for the construction of places of worship, resulting in an increasing number of religious activities taking place in China's many cities and villages. In short, clergy of the Open Church received financial support for their activities and churches. By the end of the 1980s, China had a fully functioning Catholic Church in which Mass was celebrated daily.

Yet although the Catholic Church was reborn, "religious freedom" had strict limits. Beijing made it clear that the Bureau of Religious Affairs controlled religious activities, and that the government was to administer the work of the clergy. It was understood that religious groups should be patriotic, following the instructions of the CCP and national and local government directives. In addition, Beijing maintained close scrutiny of the Underground Church. Optimists and pessimists held diametrically opposed views on the CCP's relations with the Catholic Church. Although the CCP had carried out a noticeable program of reforms, there were numerous implementation and enforcement problems, including the monitoring of religion and society.

Concerns relating to the loyalty and obedience of the Chinese people were of tremendous significance to Communist leaders. Although China implemented reforms and opened to the outside world, its cultural evolution did not keep pace with the rapid material progress that resulted from the implementation of the Four Modernizations. Although Beijing remained extremely distrustful of foreign influence in China, it was aware of the need to grant its people more freedoms, including religious freedom, to avoid threatening its material progress. In spite of this awareness, in the 1980s, Beijing was highly critical of what it saw as increasing bourgeois liberalization and spiritual pollution. As a result, while the Catholic Church was now operating openly and with official approval, the Open Church was under the control of Beijing and the CCP, which raised questions regarding the Sino–Vatican alliance encouraged by the Underground Church.

CONCLUSION

As a result of issues relating to the Vatican's support of Taiwan and Beijing's unsanctioned consecration of Catholic bishops, Sino–Vatican relations had taken on a decidedly pessimistic tone, reaching an impasse by the end of the 1980s. Increasing numbers of cultural exchanges between the clergy and government officials reflected the wishes of Chinese priests, nuns, and the laity to learn from external sources. Nevertheless, official relations between China and the Vatican throughout this decade were characterized by skepticism, resentment, and conflict.

While *exchange* was possible, *adherence* to the Vatican's wishes was inconceivable. The greatest problem was the official hierarchy of the Catholic Church in China, which precluded any hope of unity with the Vatican. This hope was further thwarted by China officially forbidding foreign intrusion and Western imperialism in its internal affairs. The history of Sino–Vatican relations is therefore characterized by issues of loyalty and the burden of China's imperial past.

NOTES

1. For example, in Cuba, see Jill I. Goldenziel, "Sanctioning Faith: Religion, State, and U.S.-Cuban Relations," *Journal of Law & Politics*, Vol. XXV (2009), pp. 181–182, 191–195; Laos, see Martin Stuart-Pox and Rod Bucknell, "Politicization of the Buddhist Sangha in Laos," *Journal of Southeast Asian Studies*, Vol. 13, No. 1 (March 1982), pp. 61–68.
2. Beatrice Leung, "China's Religious Freedom Policy: The Art of Managing Religious Activity," *China Quarterly*, No. 184 (2005), pp. 910–912; André Laliberté, "Religion and the State in China: The Limits of Institutionalization," *Journal of Current Chinese Affairs*, Vol. 40, No. 2 (2011), pp. 12–13.
3. Leung, "China's Religious Freedom Policy," p. 910.
4. Jianbo Huang, "Who Am I: Identity Tensions Among Chinese Intellectual Christians," paper presented at the annual meeting of the Association for the Sociology of Religion, San Francisco, California, August 14, 2004, http://www.hartfordinstitute.com/soc iology/huang.html (accessed July 13, 2020).
5. John Peale, *The Love of God in China: Can One Be Both Chinese and Christian?* (Bloomington: iUniverse, 2005), pp. 24–30 in particular concern this identity issue.
6. Ben Blanchard, "China Official Says West Using Christianity to 'Subvert' Power," Reuters, March 12, 2019, https://www.reu ters.com/article/us-china-parliament-religion/china-official-says-west-using-christianity-to-undermine-country-idUSKBN1QT03C (accessed July 13, 2020).
7. Rachel Xiaohong Zhu, "The Division of the Roman Catholic Church in Mainland China: History and Challenges," *Religions*, March 14, 2017, p. 9, https://doi.org/10.3390/rel8030039.
8. Bernardo Cervellera, "Religious Policy in China Before and After the Sino-Vatican Agreement," *AsiaNews.it*, December 9, 2019, http://www.asianews.it/news-en/Religious-policy-in-China-bef ore-and-after-the-Sino-Vatican-agreement-47980.html (accessed July 17, 2020).
9. Constitution of the People's Republic of China (Adopted at the Fifth Session of the Fifth National People's Congress and Promulgated for implementation by the Proclamation of the National People's Congress on December 4, 1982).

10. "Three-Self Patriotic Movement," Chinaculture.org, http://en.chi naculture.org/2014-12/01/content_579155.htm (accessed May 28, 2020).

11. Ibid., p. 346.

12. Gao Wangzhi, "Y. T. Wu: A Christian Leader Under Communism," in *Christianity in China: From the Eighteenth Century to the Present*, ed. Daniel H. Bays (Stanford, CA: Stanford University Press, 1996), pp. 343–344.

13. Willian Wan, "Prophet or Judas? Son of China's Church Founder Tackles Thorny Legacy," *The Washington Post*, September 7, 2014, https://www.washingtonpost.com/world/prophet-or-judas-son-of-chinas-church-founder-tackles-thorny-legacy/2014/09/06/9d56d584-2e8e-11e4-994d-202962a9150c_story.html (accessed July 19, 2020).

14. When Gong was released in 1985, he had already been in jail for 30 years. In 1988, Gong had a private meeting with then Pope John Paul II and learned that he had been privately named a cardinal in 1979. "Ignatius Cardinal Kung," *Encyclopaedia Britannica*, https://www.britannica.com/biography/Ignatius-Cardinal-Kung (accessed May 28, 2020); The Cardinal Kung Foundation, "Biography," http://www.cardinalkungfoundation.org/ck/CKlife.php (accessed July 19, 2020); Paul P. Mariani studies the opposition of Gong Pinmei and the Catholics in Shanghai in the 1950s in *Church Militant: Bishop Kung and Catholic Resistance in Communist Shanghai* (Cambridge: Harvard University Press, 2011).

15. Deng later wrote his memoirs, *How Inscrutable His Way!*, and provided valuable insights into the difficulties of the Shanghai Catholics. Deng was later imprisoned for 22 years. In 1981, the Pope promoted Bishop Deng, who became the Archbishop of Guangzhou, an incident that worsened Sino–Vatican relations. See Dominic Tang, S. J., *How Inscrutable His Ways! Memoirs* (Hong Kong: Dominic Tang, S.J., 1994) (available in both Chinese and English versions); Beatrice Leung and Shun-hing Chan, *Changing Church and State Relations in Hong Kong, 1950–2000* (Hong Kong: Hong Kong University Press, 2003), p. 76.

16. Jacqueline E. Wenger, "Official vs. Underground Protestant Churches in China: Challenges for Reconciliation and Social Influence," *Review of Religious Research*, Vol. 46, No. 2 (December 2004), p. 170.

17. Eric O. Hanson, "The Catholic Church in China," in *Catholicism and Politics in Communist Societies*, ed. Pedro Ramet (Durham: Duke University Press, 1990), p. 259.

18. Gao, "Y. T. Wu," p. 348.

19. Beatrice Leung, *Sino-Vatican Relations: Problems in Conflicting Authority, 1976–1986* (Cambridge University Press, 1992), p. 379.

20. Zhu, "The Division of the Roman Catholic Church," p. 6.

21. "Commentary: Document #30: True Christians and Authentic Chinese," in *Papal Documents Related to China 1937–2005*, researched and compiled by Elmer Wurth, M. M., ed. Betty Ann Maheu, M. M. (Hong Kong: Holy Spirit Study Centre, 2006), p. 187.

22. Daniel H. Bays, "China," in *The Wiley Blackwell Companion to World Christianity*, eds. Lamin Sanneh and Michael McClymond (Hoboken, NJ: Wiley & Sons, 2016), p. 538.

23. Richard Madsen, *China's Catholics: Tragedy and Hope in an Emerging Civil Society* (Berkeley: University of California Press, 1998), pp. 40–41.

24. Zhu, "The Division of the Roman Catholic Church," p. 6.

25. Kenneth L. Woodward and Melinda Liu, "Christianity Reborn in China," *Newsweek*, June 23, 1980, p. 85.

26. "Document #29: Prayers for the Great Chinese People," August 19, 1979, in *Papal Documents Related to China 1937–2005*, pp. 179–180.

27. Ibid., p. 179.

28. "A Chronology of the Catholic Church in China in the Context of Selected Dates in World and Chinese History," *Tripod*, No. 76 (July–August 1993), p. 41.

29. Ibid.

30. Ibid., p. 21.

31. John Tong, "The Church from 1949 to 1990," in *The Catholic Church in Modern China*, eds. Edmond Tang and Jean-Paul Wiest (Maryknoll, NY: Orbis Books, 1993), p. 17.

32. Ibid., pp. 17, 20–21.

33. For the CCP's united front with the Guomindang (GMD), see John W. Garver, "The Origins of the Second United Front: The Comintern and the Chinese Communist Party," *China Quarterly*, No. 113 (March 1988), pp. 29–59.

34. Jinghao Zhou, *Remaking China's Public Philosophy for the Twentieth-First Century* (Connecticut: Praeger, 2003), p. 140.

35. "Commentary: Document #30: True Christians and Authentic Chinese," in *Papal Documents Related to China 1937–2005*, p. 187.

36. "Commentary: Document #31: Letter to the Bishops of the World," in *Papal Documents Related to China 1937–2005*, p. 194.

37. Dominic Tang, S.J., *How Inscrutable His Ways! Memoirs*, 3rd enlarged ed. (Hong Kong: Condor Production, 1994), p. 199.

38. Hongyi Lai, *China's Governance Model: Flexibility and Durability of Pragmatic Authoritarianism* (London: Routledge, 2016), p. 160.

39. Jin had done much to rejuvenate the Church, but it was only on the death of his rival, an elderly bishop consecrated by Rome, that he applied to the Vatican and became a legitimate bishop of the Roman Catholic Church. The consecration of bishops has always been extremely difficult in China. See Paul P. Mariani, "The Four Catholic Bishops of Shanghai: 'Underground' and 'Patriotic' Church Competition and Sino-Vatican Relations in Reform-Era China," *Journal of Church and State*, No. 1, Vol. 58 (August 2014), pp. 42–44, https://doi.org/10.1093/jcs/csu078.

40. Charbonnier, "The Catholic Church in China," p. 314.

41. Ibid.

42. Magdaléna Masláková and Anežka Satorová, "The Catholic Church in Contemporary China: How Does the New Regulation on Religious Affairs Influence the Catholic Church?," *Religions*, July 23, 2019, pp. 7–8, 11, https://doi.org/10.3390/rel100 70446.

43. Britta Schmitz, "Christians in China—Expansion and Limitation of Churches," *KAS International Reports*, December 2010, pp. 10–13; Masláková and Satorová, "The Catholic Church in Contemporary China," pp. 10–11.

44. "Document No. 19: The Basic Viewpoint and Policy on the Religious Question During Our Country's Socialist Period," https://is.muni.cz/el/1421/jaro2011/KSCB023/um/24029748/Document_no._19_1982.pdf, (accessed July 31, 2020).
45. Ibid.
46. "What Changed at Vatican II," *The Catholic Register*, October 8, 2012, https://www.catholicregister.org/features/item/15194-what-changed-at-vatican-ii (accessed July 31, 2020); Andrew P. Lynch, "Beijing and the Vatican: Catholics in China and the Politics of Religious Freedom," *SAGE Open*, Vol. 4, No. 4 (October–December 2014), pp. 4–5.
47. Christopher S. Wren, "Chinese Catholics Rebuke the Pope," *New York Times*, March 21, 1982.
48. Daniel L. Overmyer, "Religion in China Today: Introduction," *The China Quarterly*, No. 174 (June 2003), p. 308.
49. Wren, "Chinese Catholics Rebuke the Pope," p. 9.

CHAPTER 2

The Canossian Sisters in Hong Kong and Beyond: Protection, Education, and Emancipation of Women

Gianni Criveller

Abstract Canossian nuns, in Hong Kong since 1860 (in China and Macau in 1868 and 1874), founded orphanages, schools, and hospitals (including Canossa Hospital). Women from Chinese and other background joined the Italian Sisters, making them the largest Catholic female congregation in Hong Kong. Two women were exceptionally important in the early years: Mother Lucia Cupis and Emily Bowring. The latter was the daughter of the governor and, quite sensationally, joined the Italian Canossians just a few days after their arrival. In 160 years of history, more than 530 Canossian Sisters served in education, evangelization, and care for orphans and the sick. Their impact in the field of women emancipation is without comparison, making a remarkable difference in the life of women.

G. Criveller (✉)
PIME International Missionary School of Theology, Monza, Italy

© The Author(s), under exclusive license to Springer Nature
Singapore Pte Ltd. 2022
C. Y. Chu (ed.), *The Catholic Church, The Bible, and Evangelization
in China*, Christianity in Modern China,
https://doi.org/10.1007/978-981-16-6182-2_2

21

Keywords Catholic Mission to Hong Kong · Canossian Sisters · Emily Bowring · Sacred Heart Canossian College · Canossa Hospital

Six female missionaries, known as Canossian Sisters, arrived in Hong Kong from their native Italy on April 12, 1860. They were the first arrivals of a female Catholic congregation that has done a great deal of good work in favor of the protection, education, and emancipation of women. They have done exceptional things and left an indelible mark on the history of the city. With nearly eighty members, the Canossian Sisters are now the largest female Catholic congregation in Hong Kong.

The formal name of the Canossian Sisters is the Daughters of Charity. The congregation was founded in Verona (in northern Italy) in 1808 by the Marquise Maddalena di Canossa. The congregation quickly spread throughout Veneto and Lombardy, promoting the education of poor girls and young women. The mission to Hong Kong was the first expedition of the Canossian congregation outside Italy. There was obviously a great deal of concern and anxiety over this new beginning. The Sisters were the first Italian women to settle in Hong Kong but not the first female congregation there, as the French Sisters of Saint Paul de Chartres had been in Hong Kong since 1848.

Heroic Beginnings

The six pioneering Sisters were Lucia Cupis (the superior of the group, 39 years old), Maria Stella (27), Rachele Tronconi (33), Giuseppina Testera (29), Giovanna Scotti (22), and Claudia Compagnotti (20). On February 28, 1860, they departed from Venice for Trieste, where they boarded the ship *America* and sailed to Alexandria in Egypt. From there, they boarded the *Colombo*. In Ceylon, they embarked on the *Cadiz*, a much smaller vessel that would take them to Hong Kong. It was a long and difficult journey.

In their company traveled Father Giuseppe Burghignoli of the Foreign Missions of Milan (now PIME), who was on his way to his mission in Hong Kong. Burghignoli became vicar general of the Hong Kong apostolic vicariate and an important source of support for the Canossians. The Milanese missionaries had settled in the British colony only two years earlier, in 1858. Giuseppe Marinoni, their superior in Milan, and their founder, Angelo Ramazzotti, patriarch of Venice, took the initiative of inviting the Canossians to open a mission in Asia. After considering India as a possible destination, they decided for Hong Kong.

Due to an unfortunate miscommunication, no one was waiting for the Sisters at Victoria Harbour on the morning of April 12. The letter announcing their arrival never reached Hong Kong, and therefore, no accommodation had been readied for the Sisters. It must have been a disappointment for the women after such a long and dangerous journey. Nothing was easy for them. However, the women were endowed with great courage and devotion and were ready to overcome any challenge. Among them, Lucia Cupis and Maria Stella, the first two superiors, stood out for their strong personalities: "There is no doubt that the fact that they had arrived unexpectedly and caused some uneasiness in the Sisters, but, writing to Italy, they tried their best to minimize this factor, stressing instead the warmth of the welcoming on the part of the Fathers and their sincere joy having them in Hong Kong."[1]

EMILY BOWRING, THE GOVERNOR'S DAUGHTER

A few hours after the Sisters' arrival, they met the young Emily Bowring, the favorite daughter of John Bowring, the fourth governor of Hong Kong (1854–1859). The story of Emily Bowring is an unusual one. At twenty-seven years old, she was one of the most admired women in the colony. In fact, as her mother was often sick and eventually died in England in 1857, the duty of "first lady" in the colony fell on young Emily. She was often carried around the city in the official sedan chair of the British governor. The Bowring family were the first residents of the well-known Government House, completed in 1854, which was the residence of the Hong Kong governors until 1997, since when it has been occupied by the chief executives of Hong Kong.

A few years earlier, while still in England, Emily had shocked her family by converting to Catholicism. Sir John Bowring was a Unitarian and had some anti-Catholic prejudices, as was typical at the time. Nonetheless, both Emily and another of his nine children, Charles, converted to Catholicism, with Charles becoming a Jesuit priest in Rome in 1857 while his father was serving as governor in Hong Kong. An honest man, Sir Bowring left the city in a state of disappointment, but his daughter Emily decided to stay behind in Hong Kong.[2]

Upon meeting the Sisters who had just arrived from Italy, Emily made the sensational decision to become a Canossian Sister. The missionaries were impressed by Emily and her strong yet humble personality. Sister Lucia Cupis greatly admired Emily from their very first meeting, and this admiration was sincerely reciprocated. Ida Sala narrates the first meeting of the two by quoting a letter written by Sister Cupis: "No sooner had she seen us that she burst into tears of joy, fell on her knees as if she had seen something divine, and with strong pressure of her hands, she tried to convey her feelings of affection which she could not express in words."[3]

Emily would eventually take the religious name of Aloysia in honor of her Jesuit brother, who had already passed away in Rome, and in devotion to Saint Aloysius Gonzaga. Ida Sala described quite eloquently how the worlds of Emily and the Italian Sisters could not have been more different. Emily was a self-confident and highly educated British woman belonging to a class that was then dominating the entire planet. She was brought up in luxury and had power and servants at her disposal. In contrast, the Italian Sisters were children of ordinary people. Nonetheless, their encounter was one of mutual appreciation and dedication.[4]

Emily never regretted her decision. In 1866, the Church of England missionary Matilda Sharp (after whom the Matilda Hospital at Victoria Peak in Hong Kong is named) recounted her encounter with the famous British girl turned Catholic Sister in an Italian congregation: "She was very sweet and had a happy smile and looked at peace with God and man, but still, what a life!"[5] On May 1, 1860, only seventeen days after their arrival, the Sisters inaugurated the Italian Convent School on Caine Road (now Sacred Heart Canossian College), with Emily Bowring as its first director. On May 10, with the help of two young Chinese women, the Italian Sisters founded the Pui Ching Chinese School for the assistance and education of orphans.

In 1862, they built their headquarters at 36 Caine Road. Meanwhile, they founded a boarding house for European girls, an orphanage for girls, a dispensary, a home for disabled people, and a catechumenate. In 1869, they opened the Saint Francis Community in Wan Chai, together with another school, an orphanage, a home for girls, and a hospital. Other schools for poor children were opened in 1880 in Kowloon (Bridges Street School, which operated until 1922) and in Yau Ma Tei (which closed in 1923), together with other activities for young women and poor families. More Sisters arrived in the following years: three in 1861, two in 1962, six in 1867, and three in 1869. Between 1860 and 1910, thirty expeditions left Italy for Hong Kong, bringing ninety-two Sisters to Hong Kong, Macau, and China.

The two women who greatly influenced the Canossian enterprise in Hong Kong in the crucial early years, the superior Lucia Cupis and Emily Bowring, died only a few months apart, in 1869 and 1870, respectively. They were women with strong personalities who understood and respected each other despite their vastly different backgrounds. Emily Bowring was only 37 when she died. Sister Cupis died at 49 among the general consideration that she was a saint.

Arduous Adventures in China

In 1868, Sister Lucia Cupis, with five companions from Hong Kong, opened a new mission in Wuhan (Hubei) amid unimaginable privation and difficulties. As in Hong Kong eight years earlier, poor planning on the part of the Franciscan friars responsible for the mission meant that there was no accommodation ready for the poor Sisters, who reached Wuhan after a journey full of "extraordinary adventures."[6] Sister Cupis fell sick on the first night, and poor health due to the extreme conditions she had to endure led her to her early death in 1870. Sister Cupis and her companions' determination was gravely tested but they did not give up.

Subsequently, the Canossians opened other missions in the provinces of Shaanxi, Henan, Fujian, and Guangdong. Between 1868 and 1952, 275 Sisters worked on the mainland, the majority of whom were Italian, along with a few Chinese. Between 1947 and 1952, 115 Sisters were expelled from China, and most of them continued their service among the Chinese in Hong Kong. Sister Maria Biffi was killed along with many other people taking shelter at the convent during the Japanese bombing of Huizhou on January 8, 1941.

The extraordinary story of the work of the Canossians in their 84 years in mainland China is narrated in the 590 pages of the second volume of Sala's *History of Our Canossian Missions.*[7] In these pages, the admiration for the Sisters is clear: "What they did, what they went through, is, at times, simply astonishing! But it is the truth. Not a single line of this book is fruit of my imagination. Everything is documented and everything really happened."[8] This sentiment is echoed by Ilva Fornaro: "What they achieved was simply marvelous, what they suffered simply unbelievable, their faith simply stupendous."[9]

From Hong Kong to Asia and the Rest of the World

In 1874, the Canossian Sisters settled down in Macau and more missions were opened in East Timor (1879), India (1889), Singapore (1894), Malacca/Malaysia (1905), Japan (1951), the Philippines (1963), Taiwan (1968), Australia, and even Canada (among the Chinese expatriate community).[10] For several decades, Hong Kong remained the center of arrival from Europe and of departure for different locations in mainland China and elsewhere in Asia. The Sisters thus contributed, from the very beginning, to making Hong Kong an international city.

Chinese Canossians

Numerous Chinese girls and women entered the Canossian community. Most were "tertiaries": unmarried women who dedicated themselves to the mission without public religious vows. In the first 50 years of the Canossian presence in Hong Kong (1860–1910), 66 "tertiaries" joined the institute. In 1922, Bishop Domenico Pozzoni sponsored the foundation of the Precious Blood Sisters, which was the first female-only Chinese congregation in Hong Kong.[11] Making up the bulk of this new religious group, a diocesan congregation, were the 60 tertiaries belonging to the Canossian institute. Therefore, the Precious Blood Sisters, now the second largest women's congregation in Hong Kong, are to be considered part of the Canossians' legacy.

Among the nearly 80 members of the congregation in Hong Kong today, only a few of the Sisters are Italian and most are Chinese, indicating that the Daughters of Charity have become an integral part of the local community.[12]

Canossian Hospitals

Canossa Hospital opened in April 1929, under the responsibility of Sister Teresa Pera. The hospital is still at its original site on Old Peak Road. The lot, which included a beautiful villa, was donated to the Canossians in 1925 by the English solicitor J. M. Stephens. The building was originally meant to serve as a resting home for the Sisters, but it was transformed into a hospital and became one of the most well-known health services in the territory. Agreement with the Catholic Mission established that the hospital would accept priests in need of care without charge. The building was destroyed during the Second World War and the current structure was inaugurated in 1960. In 1991, responsibility for the hospital was passed to Caritas of Hong Kong, but its name was preserved.

When Canossa Hospital began operating, the Sisters were already running Saint Francis Hospital in Wan Chai, which was founded in 1869 on land belonging to the Mission. The hospital included a structure to accommodate a group of blind girls. The Canossians have taken care of blind women since the time of Sister Stella and Bishop Timoleone Raimondi. Wan Chai Hospital also had a policy of dispensing free care to "seminarians, poor Christians and pagans recommended by the Mission."[13]

Illustrious Visitors at the Italian Convent

Caine Road has always served as the headquarters of the Canossian congregation. It includes a residence for the Sisters (known as the Italian Convent), an orphanage, Pui Ching Chinese School, and Sacred Heart School. The latter has remained the highest educational service offered by the congregation in the city. After Emily Bowring, Sister Maria Allanson, the daughter of an English father and a Portuguese mother, took over as director of the school with great competence until 1908. In 1910, the English school had 286 pupils, Pui Ching school had 89, and the orphanage accommodated 263 orphans (girls from both Eurasian and Chinese backgrounds).

On December 4, 1933, the convent received a visit from the famous Italian scientist Guglielmo Marconi and his wife.[14] Another illustrious visit was on April 12, 1934, when Archbishop Mario Zanin, the apostolic delegate to China, visited the convent and the schools and was received with all honors. The principal of the school, Sister Mabel Anderson, chose a nicely dressed fourteen-year-old girl to present the bouquet of flowers to the guest. The little girl was born in Macau and was not a Christian, but she was proud to be given the privilege, which she spoke of many times later. After this occasion, she had the highest respect for the Sisters. Years later, she had to move to Guangzhou because of the Japanese invasion. Widowed with small children, she was in a state of great difficulty and decided to pass from leaning toward faith to actually receiving baptism. One of her children entered the seminary and became priest and bishop; he is Cardinal John Tong, the incumbent apostolic administrator of Hong Kong. I was told of this private episode, which I report here with affection, by the cardinal himself.[15]

An Educational and Charitable Legacy

Although there is more to tell, the barriers to accessing sources during this difficult period of the pandemic prevent me from expanding the scope of my narrative. In conclusion, since their early days in Hong Kong, the Canossians have been a center of educational, social, and evangelizing activity, continuously developing in accordance with the changing needs of the local society. With the strength of their faith and determination, the first pioneers with Emily Bowring and their successors brought hope and relief to many in Hong Kong, in the face of epidemics, natural disasters, and a challenging social environment. They rescued thousands of girls from certain death and trained generations of young women who would influence all sectors of society: religious, social, cultural, entrepreneurial, and political.

This has been made possible by the strong personalities of the missionaries, animated by exceptional faith and determination. Their dedication and generosity are beyond words. More than a few of them succumbed to fatigue and poor health at a young age. The number of Canossians who died young, at least in the early decades of their mission, can be recognized by visiting the tomb monument in the Happy Valley Cemetery in Hong Kong. On the top of that list is Giovanna Scotti, part of the first expedition, who died at the age of 29. More Sisters died young in the subsequent years, each time inflicting a great emotional blow to the small community. From 1896 to 1939, 24 Sisters died of infectious diseases while they were serving the sick in Hong Kong and China. Epidemics, natural disasters, shipwrecks, persecutions, and misunderstandings (even by ecclesiastical superiors) marked their difficult and exacting mission.

After the Second World War, as mentioned above, many Canossian Sisters who were expelled from mainland China came to Hong Kong and Macau, together with more than a million refugees. Education became the most urgent need for the large number of young refugees. The Canossians founded over 20 new schools, giving particular priority to girls from poor families. One of these was Canossa Primary School in Wong Tai Shin, which was opened in 1969 on the request of Bishop Lorenzo Bianchi. This school was especially aimed at including the children of police officers, who were in great distress after the 1967 riots.[16]

In its 160 years of history, more than 530 Canossian Sisters of Italian, Chinese, British, Portuguese, and other nationalities served in Hong Kong and Macau, working in the fields of education, evangelization, and the care of orphans and the sick. The Canossian Sisters continue their mission in Hong Kong and Macau today, administering some of the most respected educational and health institutions in the two territories. The impact of their presence in these societies is remarkable and is well above that of other institutions in the field of women's education.

I take the liberty of mentioning that in April 2020, on the invitation of the Italian General Consul, I wrote an article[17] and recorded a video[18] about the Canossian Sisters in Hong Kong. Since these were published, I have received many messages from Hong Kong women telling me how the Canossian Sisters and the schools run by them have touched their lives. This was a small confirmation of the remarkable difference that the Canossians have made in the lives of thousands of women. They are greatly respected by the Catholic community and by the society as a whole.

NOTES

1. Ida Sala, *History of Our Canossian Missions*, vol. 1 (Hong Kong: Canossian Missions, FdCC, 1997), p. 85.
2. For the remarkable story of Emily Bowring, see Nora M. Clarke and Lina Riva, *The Governor's Daughter Takes the Veil, Sister Aloysia Emily Bowring, Canossian Daughter of Charity* (Hong Kong: Caritas, 1980).
3. Sala, *History of Our Canossian Missions*, vol. 1, p. 95. The quotation is from a letter by Cupis to Sister Lucca dated February 14, 1860.
4. Sala dedicates many eloquent pages to Emily's entrance into the Canossian congregation, ibid., pp. 87–104.
5. Ibid., p. 95, quoting from Joyce Stevens Smith, *Matilda: A Hong Kong Legacy* (Hong Kong, 1988).
6. Ibid., p. 185. The quotation is from a letter by Cupis to Raimondi dated August 12, 1868.
7. Ida Sala, *History of Our Canossian Missions*, vol. 2 (Hong Kong: Canossian Missions, FdCC, 1999).
8. Ibid., p. ii
9. Ibid., p. i.

10. *Five Loaves and Two Fishes. Canossian Mission to the Far East (1860–2010)* (Hong Kong: Canossian Daughters of Charity, 2010), pp. 12, 20, 37, 42.

11. See Cindy Yik-yi Chu, *The Chinese Sisters of the Precious Blood and the Evolution of the Catholic Church* (Palgrave Macmillan, 2017).

12. *Hong Kong Catholic Church Directory* (Hong Kong: Catholic Truth Society, 2019), pp.188–191.

13. Ida Sala, *History of Our Canossian Missions*, vol. 3 (Hong Kong: Canossian Missions, FdCC, 2003), p. 41.

14. Ibid., p. 52.

15. Gianni Criveller, "Interview with Bishop John Tong," *Tripod* 153 (2009), pp. 5–18.

16. Sala, *History of Our Canossian Missions*, vol. 3, pp. 212–13.

17. Gianni Criveller, "A Quiet Arrival with a Huge Impact: the Canossian Sisters in Hong Kong," *Sunday Examiner*, April 20, 2020.

18. Consulate General of Italy in Hong Kong, "How Six Young Canossian Sisters from Italy made a Remarkable Contribution to the History of Hong Kong," *Facebook*, April 12, 2020, https://www.facebook.com/ItalianConsulate.HK/posts/2504637263120251.

PART II

The Bible

CHAPTER 3

Reading and Praying with the Studium Biblicum Version (*Sigao Shengjing*)

Raissa De Gruttola

Abstract The contents of the Bible are central for the life of a Christian community, and a clear and faithful translation of the original message is necessary to convey it to the faithful. The first complete Catholic Bible in Chinese was published in 1968 and, subsequently, other translations of the Chinese Bible have been published, while the significant role of the Bible has been constantly supported and enhanced by other texts, both translated and directly written in the Chinese language. In this chapter, two Chinese versions of the Gospel of John will be analyzed to explore the features of the two volumes the Studium Biblicum Version (*Sigao Shengjing* 1968) and *Xinyue Shengjing* (2014). The history of the two translations will be presented and the structure of the text will be analyzed.

R. De Gruttola (✉)
University of Perugia, Perugia, Italy
e-mail: raissa.degruttola@unipg.it

© The Author(s), under exclusive license to Springer Nature
Singapore Pte Ltd. 2022
C. Y. Chu (ed.), *The Catholic Church, The Bible, and Evangelization in China*, Christianity in Modern China,
https://doi.org/10.1007/978-981-16-6182-2_3

33

Keywords Chinese Bible · Christianity in China · Bible translation ·
Claretian new testament · *Sigao Shengjing*

The first complete translation of the Catholic Bible in the Chinese
language, published in 11 volumes, was only completed in 1961. The
translation was published in 1968 in a single volume edition and is known
by the name the Studium Biblicum Version, so *Sigao Shengjing* 思高圣经.
In 1969, the text was approved by the Congregation for Divine Worship
as the official version to be used in Catholic liturgical celebrations given
in the Chinese language. Nevertheless, in the following years, together
with periodical reviews of the Studium Biblicum Version, new Bible translations were made available for Chinese Catholics and new publishing
houses committed themselves to printing and distributing Catholic books
and texts in Chinese. These texts and their contents are now also circulated via websites and mobile applications, thus providing believers with
easily accessible means by which to stay connected with the Word of God.
The supporting role of the introductions and notes is particularly important and, for many Bible editions, is the element that marks the difference
between the Catholic and Protestant approaches to the Holy Scripture,
especially in its Chinese translations, with the former largely permitting
the use of explanatory matter alongside the biblical text and the latter
preferring to avoid the presence of notes, believing "in the sufficiency of
the Scriptures to carry light to the soul."[1]

In this chapter, after a brief presentation of the historical background
of Bible translation in China and the translation process of the Studium
Biblicum Version, another version of the Bible is analyzed: the New
Testament published by the Claretian Press (hereafter the Claretian
New Testament). This translation, available since 2014, has some pecu-
liar features worthy of exploration and comparison with the Studium
Biblicum Version, published by the Franciscan friars of the Studium
Biblicum Franciscanum Sinense.

In this chapter, the Studium Biblicum Version and Claretian New
Testament versions of the Gospel of John are analyzed to explore similarities and differences, in terms of both the translation of the text itself
and of additional notes and explanatory matter, which constitute fundamental elements in both volumes. Other aspects of the editorial work
of both publishing houses are also presented, with the aim of exploring

what other contemporary tools support the knowledge and comprehension of the Catholic faithful with regard to biblical content in the Chinese language. To conclude, some references are made to the importance of paratextual matter in Bible translation and its function for different types of readers and in different editions.

THE STUDIUM BIBLICUM VERSION AND THE CLARETIAN NEW TESTAMENT

When the Italian Franciscan Gabriele Allegra (真福雷永明神父 1907–1976) asked the permission of his superiors to become a missionary to China in 1931, it was with the principal purpose of translating the Catholic Scriptures into the Chinese language. At the beginning of the twentieth century, the Chinese faithful still lacked a complete version of the Catholic Bible in their language. Of course, this did not mean that there were not Catholic texts translated into the Chinese language, including partial translations of the Holy Scripture. The Jesuit missionaries of the seventeenth century undertook translation projects and wrote and circulated Catholic texts in Chinese. However, although these included catechisms, books on the sacraments, books with prayers, lives of saints, collections of parables, episodes of the life of Jesus, and the most important biblical stories, they did not include a complete Bible. The Jesuits' decision to prioritize the translation and publication of other types of texts was, of course, a reflection of the attitude assumed by the Church in Rome, and in all other mission areas, toward the Scriptures and their languages. In fact, after the Council of Trent (1545–1563), the Catholic Church hierarchy admitted the Latin-language *Vulgate* as the only official biblical text and established that translation into other modern languages would not be permitted. As such, when missionaries from Europe reached other countries and started to talk and write about Christianity in those places, the official liturgy and official texts were always in Latin, although local languages could be used for oral preaching and explanations, and for catechisms and other texts.

This background makes clear the reasons for the lack of a complete edition of the Catholic Bible in Chinese. That Father Allegra had the opportunity to accomplish his project at the beginning of the twentieth century was due to changes in the attitude of the Universal Church toward the use and translation of the Scriptures. Before the Second Vatican Council (1962–1965), other official documents had addressed the issue of Bible translation and prepared the context in which Father Allegra could be supported in his task by his superiors and the Church hierarchy.

Gabriele Allegra arrived in China in 1931 and started his translation of the Old Testament 4 years later. Working alone, he translated each book from the original Hebrew texts. This aspect is remarkable, as all of the previous translation attempts made by Catholic missionaries were based on the Latin text, and the majority of the Protestant translations were based on the most authoritative English versions, representing in most cases examples of indirect translation.[2] This gave Allegra's translation a new, more scientific status.

When the translation of the Old Testament was complete, Father Allegra created a team of Chinese Franciscan friars to revise the whole text and prepare an introduction and notes for each book. These were the first members of the Studium Biblicum Franciscanum Sinense (hereafter Studium Biblicum), otherwise known as the Sigao Shengjing Xuehui 思高圣经学会 (Scotus Bible Association), an institute founded by Allegra in 1945 to deal with the translation and circulation of the Bible in the Chinese language. The eight volumes of the Old Testament were published from 1946 to 1954 in Beijing and Hong Kong (where the Sigao Shengjing Xuehui moved in 1948). The translation of the New Testament then began, with some books assigned to small teams made up of two or three members of the institute. The New Testament was translated and published between 1957 and 1961. From 1961 to 1968, a complete revision of each book was made by the friars with the aim of preparing a single-volume edition, which was published and distributed on Christmas Day in 1968. One year later, the volume was approved by the Congregation for Divine Worship as the official version to be used in Catholic liturgical celebrations. Nevertheless, it was not yet possible to circulate the volume in mainland China, where, throughout almost the entirety of the twentieth century, the New Testament edition used was the *Xinjing Quanji* 新经全集 by the Jesuit Xiao Jingshan 萧静山, which was translated from the Latin *Vulgate* and first printed in 1922. In the following decades, the *Xinjing Quanji* was revised and republished; in 1990, it was distributed together with the Studium Biblicum Old Testament, and only in 1992 was the complete the Studium Biblicum Version printed and distributed in Beijing.[3]

The printed edition of the Studium Biblicum Version available today is the result of further revisions, but it preserves the introduction to each book, the translated text, the numerous footnotes, and the rich paratextual matter, which strongly support individual readers in their understanding and the priests, catechists, and preachers who have to explain the content to groups of listeners, both believers and non-believers. A precious element found on each page of the volume is the intertextual references, indicating in which other parts of the Bible particular sentences, content, or keywords can also be found. The intertextual references are a feature typical of the "Jerusalem Bible"; in light of their widely acknowledged usefulness, the Studium Biblicum members decided to include them in their version, and they are also retained in the online version of the translation (which is discussed below).

In 1998, the first edition of the Chinese Pastoral Bible was published in Hong Kong under the title *Muling Shengjing* 牧灵圣经.[4] It was based on the Spanish text of *La Biblia Latinoamericana*, a translation made by Father Bernard Hurault (于贺神父1924–2004) and published in South America in the 1970s with the purpose of providing the unlearned with a simple text written in an easy language that they could understand with the aid of explanatory notes. The project to produce a Chinese Pastoral Bible had the same aim. The 1998 edition was revised several times before a completely new translation was started in 2006, and in 2014, the Claretian New Testament was published in Macau.[5] A precious part of this volume is the section *Lectio Divina* (*Xie Zhu du jing* 偕主读经) or "divine reading" (literally "reading the Scripture with the Lord"), the features of which help the reader understand the aim of the whole translation method.

Five short chapters precede the text of the translated New Testament, and one of the most relevant among these is an explanation of the *Lectio Divina* written by the Jesuit Father Mark Fang Zhirong 房志荣. In another section, after an overview of the history of the translations of the Catholic Bible into Chinese, it is stated that "there cannot be a perfect translation,"[6] and different translation methods are presented. Here, it is necessary to briefly recall the concept of dynamic equivalence expressed by Eugene Nida, according to which a good translation must be able to reproduce in its reader the same feelings that arise in the reader of the original text.[7] The concluding paragraph describes the features of the 2014 Claretian New Testament: "This is a translation according to partial dynamic equivalence, the translated text of the four Gospels is simple but not weakened in its meaning; each Epistle has its own explanation, to help the reader to understand the richness of the original text or the differences in the translation."[8] The text continues by underlining that every passage has notes meant to help readers pray with and meditate on the Word of God and to answer to this Word in the present time and place, to strengthen their faith and gain truth and love in their life.[9]

In the chapter on praying with the Scriptures, known as the *Lectio Divina*, the structure of the process is given and each paragraph is explained and commented on so that "many readers can understand the intended meaning and profundity of every paragraph of the Bible, and it is especially suitable for new believers or those readers interested in knowing the Bible."[10] The chapter continues by presenting to the reader the best ways of and attitudes toward reading the Bible and offering some advice on using the text in contexts different from the Mass, proposing that one should invoke the Holy Spirit, read a short passage, meditate on it, and be thankful in the concluding prayer.

In the Claretian New Testament, a short introduction is given at the beginning of every book, presenting the historical background of the text, the author, and the main features of the text. Along with the translations of the New Testament, there are three other important sections. Numbered footnotes on each page explain in a very wide context the meaning of the respective group of verses. These notes very often make reference to the original texts or to other Chinese or different modern-language translations, to put the translation choices in a wider context. Smaller entries at the bottom of each page indicate the intertextual references on a verse-by-verse basis. The most interesting section, however, is the columns on the outer side of each page, where four indications can be found: *songdu* 诵读 (read), *qidao* 祈祷 (pray), *xingdong* 行动 (act), and *fanxing* 反省 (introspect).[11]

Textual Analysis

The selection of the words and passages to analyze in this chapter was made according to a previous study by the author on translation issues in the Gospel of John in the Studium Biblicum Version. The translation of these elements in the Studium Biblicum Version and in the Claretian New Testament is presented together with innovative elements from the *Lectio Divina*.[12] When referring to the text of the Studium Biblicum Version, three contemporary versions were analyzed and every passage was compared to the Gospel volume published in 1957, with any differences reported on when they occur.[13]

From this deep analysis of the Prologue of the Gospel of John, including the theological implications connected with it and the choice of some terms or syntactical structures, only a few elements are considered here. First, the word chosen to translate the Greek *logos* is *shengyan* 圣言. The translation of this concept has been debated at length in the past, leading missionaries to adopt different translations, such as *dao* 道, *wu'erpeng* 物尔朋, and *yan* 言.[14] However, the Claretian New Testament makes no reference to this matter, although the issue of the "Word being with God and the Word being God" is addressed in the footnotes. In the online version of the Studium Biblicum Version, the issue is not mentioned; in the printed edition, there is a short footnote on the matter. However, in the 1957 version of the book of the Gospels, a long endnote and a specific appendix address both the translation and meaning of *logos*. An innovative and interesting element included in the Claretian New Testament is a column reporting the phases of the *Lectio Divina*. It concerns the verses of the Prologue (1:1–18) and is divided into the four sections mentioned above. In the *songdu* entry, the theological theme of Jesus as the Word of God coming among men to bring the light is introduced, concluding that "the Prologue is written in a poetic literary style and can be understood deeply only if read repeatedly."[15] The *fanxing* entry proposes some questions:

> Which relation is between the Word and God? What kind of relationship has the Word that became flesh with men? Try to put your name in the text where "John" is found and read again: how does it make you feel?[16]

The *qidao* entry reads:

> Through the Holy Son, Christians can pray to the Holy Father. Give thanks to God for having sent his son as a present to men, and ask the Holy Spirit to accompany you in knowing this Word of God.[17]

The intertextual references in the entry at the bottom of the page in the Claretian New Testament are almost the same as those found in the Studium Biblicum Version.

It is not possible to analyze here all of the differences in the two translations of the Prologue, but it is worth noting some examples of the choices of the translators and their reasons for making these choices. In many verses, the Claretian New Testament seems clearer and easier to understand, without changing the inner meaning of the transmitted text. The Studium Biblicum Version, owing to its strict adherence to the Greek text, sometimes seems relatively obscure. Some of the strategies used to simplify the sentences in the Claretian New Testament are very simple, including the substitution of pronouns for repeated names and the addition of adverbs or conjunctions to clarify the message (Table 3.1).

Despite the common use of "Christ" to refer to Jesus Christ, almost as if this were a proper name or surname, it must be underlined that the Greek origin of the word *Christos* transmits a specific meaning: "anointed." The Greek word *Messias* translates the Hebrew word *Masiah*, which has the same meaning.[18] It is known that:

> In the New Testament, the word Christ is used in two different ways, namely, to indicate that Jesus is "the anointed one," or as part of the name of Jesus itself. What denotes the different use of the word "Christ" in the Greek text is the presence of the determinative article *ho*. In the Greek Gospel of John, the term *Christos* is found 19 times, while *Messias* occurs only twice (1:41; 4:25). In 1:41 and 4:25, where *Messias* occurs, the Greek text provides the explanation of this Hebrew word, specifying its meaning as "the Anointed." […] In these two points the Greek text does not express the article, as the word "Christ" only generally explains the meaning of Messiah as "the man chosen by God." In the other occurrences of *Christos* in the Gospel of John, the word is always preceded by the article *ho*, except for the cases 1:17 and 17:3 where, however, it is found next to the name

Table 3.1 Simplification strategies in the Claretian New Testament

Verse	The Studium Biblicum Version (Sigao Shengjing) 思高圣经	The Claretian New Testament 乐仁新约	The new American Bible (in English)
1:4	在他内有生命, 这生命是人的光。	在圣言内有生命, 这生命就是人的光。	through him was life, and this life was the light of the human race;
1:12	但是, 凡接受他的, 他给他们, 即给那些信他名字的人权能, 好成为天主的子女。	但是, 凡接受祂的, 祂赐他们权能, 成为天主的儿女, 因为他们信他名。	But to those who did accept him he gave power to become children of God, to those who believe in his name.

Iesous and does not indicate a title of Jesus, but is juxtaposed to the name as if it were a surname. In the Chinese version of the Gospel of John by the Studium Biblicum Franciscanum, both in the edition of 1957 and of 1968, in all the other occurrences of the word *Christos*, it being preceded by the article in the Greek text, it is translated with *Moxiya* instead of *Jidu*. This choice highlights a very accurate method of translation because, with the Chinese language lacking in articles, it would be very easy to misinterpret the word Jidu as simply a name of Jesus. Using the word *Moxiya*, Allegra retrieved the meaning of the word *Christos*, conveying the correct sense to the reader without distorting the original content of the text. [...] The link between the two words in Chinese is not explained in the notes in the Gospel of John, however, it is reported in the note when the word *Christos* first appears in the whole volume of the Gospel, namely in verse 22:42 of the Gospel of Matthew.[19]

This choice is not replicated in the Claretian New Testament: in all of the verses where "Christ" is found the translation is *Jidu*, although at the first occurrence (1:20) a footnote explains the equivalence of the terms and the meaning of the word *Moxiya*, and in each occurrence of the word an asterisk is placed in the text indicating a footnote that refers to the first footnote of 1:21. This reads as, "Also translated as *Moxiya*. In the Greek language *Christos*, as the Hebrew and Aramaic *Masiah*, means 'who receives instruction.'"[20] The decision to use the most common *Jidu* instead of the clearly foreign *Moxiya* reveals the intention of the translators of the Claretian New Testament to provide readers with an easily accessible text. Nonetheless, the presence of simple but important footnotes shows the attention given to the original text and to other authoritative Chinese translations.[21]

The rendering of weights, measures, and currency units in the Claretian New Testament is interesting. In the Studium Biblicum Version, together with footnotes in the text, specific tables in the paratextual matter indicate the equivalence and the value of each transliterated measure found in the text. In the Claretian New Testament, the three units found in the Gospel of John are all included in the footnotes. The cases of this are in verses 2:6; 12:3,5; 6:19; and 11:18. In verse 2:3, *yibai gongsheng* 一百公升 is given as the translation of "two or three *measures*," where a "measure" was around 45 liters. This information is given in the footnote. The same is found in verse 12:3, where the unit given in

Chinese is *dayue ban gongsheng* 大约半公升, used to measure the quantity of aromatic nard: "half a liter." Even in this passage, the footnote explains the equivalence.[22]

An interesting difference is found in verses 5:20 and 21:15–17. The original Greek text in these passages has two verbs to express two types of love and affection: *phileo* and *agapao*, where *phileo* refers to a feeling of friendship and *agapao* to the unconditional love of God. The translators of the Claretian New Testament decided to use the Chinese *xi'ai* 喜爱 to translate *agapao*, with the purpose of highlighting its difference from *ai* 爱, which is used to translate *phileo*. This choice is explained in a footnote in both occurrences. The difference between these verbs can often be used in preaching or catechesis to emphasize both the difference between human and divine feelings and the relationship between Peter and Jesus, as the occurrences in Chapter 21 refer to a dialogue between the two. The two different verbs in the Greek text of this episode are both translated as *ai* in the Studium Biblicum Version; the attached footnote addresses only the topic of the thrice repetition of the question and does not mention the use of different verbs.

Other Editorial and Online Activities

When Father Allegra founded the Studium Biblicum, the project was that of giving to the Chinese-speaking Catholic world a center for accomplishing biblical work and where the activity of circulating biblical material in the Chinese language could be undertaken. After Allegra's death, there were some difficulties in continuing to operate the Studium Biblicum; nevertheless, its activities continue today. Since 1975, a biblical dictionary and other volumes have been published. In 2016, a complete revision of the biblical text was made available. In 2012, the institute was involved in a digitalization project of some handwritten documents in collaboration with Hong Kong Baptist University and Yale University, and today, it continues to publish and distribute a biblical periodical called *Shengjing jikan* 圣经季刊 (Bible Quarterly).[23]

The Studium Biblicum Version is available through a free mobile phone application of the same name, and a Studium Biblicum Facebook group was created in 2012, which today has over 4,000 members. The Facebook group is constantly updated and shares events of the Studium Biblicum and of the Hong Kong Diocese; it posts news about the publications of the institute and written or video comments to the readings of the

Holy Mass. The Studium Biblicum also manages an official website with many interesting sections.[24] It was recently reorganized and renovated and can be consulted in traditional and simplified Chinese characters.[25] It includes sections on the history and foundation of the institute, biographical pages on Father Gabriele Allegra and Father John Duns Scotus, and contact and news sections. It also presents all of the publications of the Studium Biblicum, and there is an important section entitled "Biblical Prayer" (*Shengjing qidao* 圣言祈祷) where the Word of God can be consulted in many different ways. In the first place, the whole Bible, as translated, published, and revised by the members of the institute, is available and can be read by choosing the specific book and chapter through dedicated links. Another section presents daily meditations on short biblical passages,[26] and there are links to the daily readings of the website of the Hong Kong Catholic Diocesan Liturgy Commission (www.catholic-dlc.org.hk); another section includes the Sunday homilies by Bishop Joseph Ha Chi-shing, OFM 夏志诚主教 in video format, and those by the Franciscan Father Hu Jianting 胡健挺神父 in written files. A further section presents short meditations on Sunday readings, and another includes an explanation of the way of praying through the *Lectio Divina* according to different sources.[27]

Alongside the biblical translation with comments and guidelines for the *Lectio Divina*, the Claretian Press is also involved in other projects, such as the translation and printing of other texts with the purpose of transmitting the biblical contents to as many people as possible and through the most accessible means. For example, some relevant books that Claretian has published in Chinese are a biography of Pope Francis, *Laizi shijie jintou de jiaozong Fangji* 来自世界尽头的教宗方济 (Francis, the Pope from the End of the World),[28] and the Apostolic exhortation *Evangelii gaudium* (The Joy of the Gospel).[29] In 2019, a tour guide of the Holy Land was printed and distributed under the title *Dai ni zoujin Shengdi* 带你走进圣地 (A Pilgrim's Guide to the Holy Land) with the aim of giving Chinese-speaking pilgrims to the Holy Land a precious guide to visit the places where the events described in the Gospel took place. Since 2012, this publishing house has also published annually a small book, the *Meiri Shengyan* 每日聖言 (Bible Diary, literally "The Daily Holy Word"), with a whole year of daily Bible readings, commentaries, reflections, and prayers in the Chinese language. The Claretian Press also manages a Facebook account where news and updates are posted. The official Facebook page of the publishing house has recently began promoting the upcoming publication of the 2021 edition of the *Meiri Shengyan*.[30]

CONCLUSION

Chen Jianming recalls the statement of the French Jesuit Louis Antoine de Poirot (1735–1813):

> There were two types of reader of Scripture: those who sought moral instruction, and who did not care whether the translation was elegant or coarse, involved or abstruse, but who would still read diligently; and those who read to ease boredom, or who read for the novelty value, or to appreciate the literary quality of the writing.[31]

This statement is important to set the context for the analysis presented in this chapter. In both cases, the aim of translation is to communicate some aspects of faith; as such, the reader is not expected to be preoccupied with the elegance of the text. According to the results presented, and allowing for the research being at a preliminary stage, it is evident that the different translation choices found in the Studium Biblicum Version and the Claretian New Testament clearly correspond to the perspective of *Skopostheorie*. Leaving extensive analysis of this theory to the bibliographical reference below,[32] it is necessary here only to underline that it refers to the main and last aim of a translated text. In particular, quoting Cheung, "in Bible translation, a target text might be considered to have a missionary purpose or liturgical purpose."[33] However, this chapter shows how missionary and liturgical purposes can already be different, and that Bible translation can have other aims, such as catechesis, deepening the knowledge of Christianity, or strengthening the faith of the already baptized. Furthermore, this definition seems limited if the texts translated or written by the Jesuits in the seventeenth century, already mentioned above, are taken into account, as these show that the same purposes can be achieved through other means and through the use of other texts. In fact, on the inner nature of the biblical text and its possibility of being used as a missionary tool, the Italian Bible scholar Buzzetti underlined, "The nature of the Bible is not such as it can be directly used as an efficacious missionary or apologetic instrument [...] it is not regarded as means of communication for those who are unbelievers, but rather as a collection of texts recording, remembering, and expressing the historical moments of faith [...] a common use of the Bible may be otherwise indicated – such as, for example, in preaching – only prior to thorough knowledge of the focal elements of faith itself."[34]

Along with the translation of some extracts from the Gospel of John, this chapter considers the notes and references in the two editions, thereby recalling the importance of the paratext in biblical translation, as underlined by An-Ting Yi.[35] According to Yi,

> Footnotes and interlinear notes in Bible versions are not trivial features as many have long perceived. Instead, they can offer a fresh look at those versions as well as their contexts, *skopoi*, and translation decisions.[36]

The translators of the Studium Biblicum were aware of the importance of paratext, and the first 11 bulky volumes of translation that they published were very rich in notes and explanations. According to Father Allegra, the contents of the commentaries had to adhere to Catholic doctrine, with the aim of reporting "the voice of the Church" and the "clear and theologically solid exposition of the Sacred Text,"[37] so that they can be regarded as a "translation of the existing Catholic exegesis."[38] In fact, despite the necessity of shortening the paratextual matter to fit the logistic parameters of a single-volume edition, the most important notes, appendices, and tables were retained in the 1968 version. It seems that Allegra and his collaborators learned from the experience of Protestant Bible translation projects, which, for many editions, had applied the "without note or comment" principle. As George Mak recalls,

> To solicit support from different Protestant denominations by avoiding sectarian or theological controversy, the founders of the BFBS [British and Foreign Bible Society] agreed unanimously to exclude any note or comment of a doctrinal or practical character from the Bibles it published and distributed. [...] The BFBS's optimistic view that the Bible is self-interpreting to uninstructed non-Christian peoples was challenged by the missionary experience of China. Personal, direct contact with the Chinese people informed Protestant missionaries that the Chinese Bible was not self-interpreting to the Chinese who had no previous Christian experience, owing to cultural and religious discrepancies between Chinese society and those depicted in the Bible.[39]

These words refer to the attitude of the Protestant Bible society, which had printed the highest number of Chinese Bibles by the end of the nineteenth and the beginning of the twentieth centuries, and clearly express the relevance of explanations to the text when translating for very different cultures. It is evident that paratextual matter also had a fundamental role for the translators of the Claretian New Testament, in which it can be said that the notes and comments play a double role. In the first place, they represent, as usual, the tool through which more is communicated about the text, its contents, the original versions, and possible other interpretations, but in this case the boxes presenting indications to pray with the method of the *Lectio Divina* are also a precious help for the believer who wants to make a further step in their experience of knowing and praying with the Word of God.

The sections of the Claretian New Testament analyzed here are important both for individual use and for presenting the text to new people interested in the Catholic faith, whereas the more accurate style of translation of the Studium Biblicum Version makes it more suitable for official use during liturgies and other formal occasions. In both cases, however, the presence of a rich paratext is fundamental to the overall effectiveness of the texts.

NOTES

1. "Bible Society Speech at the Shanghai Conference," *The Bible Society Monthly Reporter* 1891, p. 151, BFBS Archives BSA/G1/3, quoted in George Kam Wah Mak, "To Add or not to Add? The British and Foreign Bible Society's Defence of the 'Without Note or Comment' Principle in Late Qing China," *Journal of the Royal Asiatic Society*, Vol. 25, No. 2 (2015), p. 336, n. 48.

2. The English origin of the Protestant missionaries is clear even when analyzing the sound of the translation of many proper names in the Bible, with the English pronunciation of Hebrew or Greek names being transferred to the choice of the Chinese syllables for the transliteration. One of the most evident cases is the name of St. Peter, sounding *Petros* in the Greek New Testament and *Bide* 彼得 in Chinese according to the English *Peter*. On the contrary, the transliteration of proper names in the Catholic texts often reveals the Latin pronunciation of the words, which is very close to the Greek. For further examples, see Raissa De Gruttola, "'And the Word Became Chinese.' Gabriele Allegra and the Chinese Catholic

Bible: History, Process, and Translation Analysis," Ph.D. diss. Ca' Foscari University of Venice, 2017, p. 137.

3. On this issue and the problems concerning vertical or horizontal typesetting and the use of traditional or simplified Chinese characters, see John Baptist Zhang Shijiang, "The Promotion of the Bible in Contemporary China and Evangelization," *Tripod*, Vol. 27, No. 144 (2007), pp. 11–21.

4. *Muling Shengjing* 牧灵圣经 (Pastoral Bible) (Hong Kong: Tianzhujiao guoji Shengjing xuehui, 1998).

5. *Xinyue Shengjing* 新约圣经 (New Testament) (Macau: Leren Chubanshe, 2014).

6. Ibid., p. x.

7. Eugene A. Nida and Charles R. Taber, *The Theory and Practice of Translation, with Special Reference to Bible Translating* (Leiden: Brill, 1969).

8. *Xinyue Shengjing*, p. xi.

9. Ibid.

10. Ibid., pp. xii–xiii.

11. Examples of the contents of these sections are given in the next paragraph. They follow the four passages of the traditional Catholic *Lectio Divina*: *lectio* (read), *meditatio* (meditate), *oratio* (pray), and *contemplatio* (contemplate), together with the final indication, *action* (act). In the section on the *Lectio Divina* of the Studium Biblicum website, these phases of the prayer with this method have different names: *songdu* 诵读 is *lectio*, *moxiang* 默想 is *meditation*, *qidao* 祈祷 is *oratio*, and *mo guan* 默观 is *contemplatio*.

12. As stated in De Gruttola, "'And the Word Became Chinese,'" p. 143, the proper names in the Gospel of John are the same in the 1968 the Studium Biblicum Version and in the 2014 Claretian New Testament. This is important in showing the intent to create uniformity in the set of proper names occurring in the Bible or referring to Christianity.

13. The translations available online on the Studium Biblicum website are a 1999 re-edition of the 1968 volume in vertical layout printed in Hong Kong in traditional Chinese characters, and a 2009 version printed in Nanjing in horizontal layout with simplified Chinese characters.

14. On this topic, see De Gruttola, "'And the Word Became Chinese,'" p. 129 and references.

15. *Xinyue Shengjing*, p. 22.
16. Ibid.
17. Ibid., p. 23.
18. From this word came also the English "Messiah," again with the meaning of "anointed" with reference to the election of priests, kings, and prophets.
19. De Gruttola, "'And the Word Became Chinese,'" pp. 130–132.
20. *Xinyue Shengjing*, p. 224.
21. A similar case is found in verse 1:34 where the translation is "*shi Tianzhu suo texuan de* 是天主所特选的" (is the one chosen by God) and the asterisk points to a footnote reading that other versions have "*Tianzhu zi* 天主子" (son of God).
22. The same process is found when translating the currency *denarius* in verse 12:5 and the length measure *stade* in verses 6:19 and 11:18.
23. This biblical journal was first released in 1977 with the name *Shengjing shuangyuekan* 圣经双月刊 (Bible Bimonthly). It was printed bimonthly up to 1998, and in 1999, it became a quarterly and took the name of *Shengjing jikan*. It covers many biblical topics and also Mariological and Franciscan issues.
24. http://www.sbofmhk.org (accessed August 5, 2020).
25. The website was renovated on July 21, 2020.
26. At the end of each meditation, it is specified that they are translated from the reflections shared through the website of the American Lay Association Our Lady of Presentation Communities and Ministries; see www.presentationministries.com/ (accessed August 10, 2020).
27. These are the Italian Cardinal Carlo Maria Martini, the Hong Kong Holy Spirit Study Centre, the Episcopal Conference of Taiwan, and the John Duns Scotus Bible Reading Promotion Center (Franciscans in Taiwan). See http://www.sbofmhk.org/pub/body/cpray/c8_lectio_divina/index.html (accessed August 10, 2020).
28. José Ruíz Márquez, *Laizi shijie jintou de jiaozong Fangji* 来自世界尽头的教宗方济 (Francis, the Pope from the End of the World) (Macau: Leren chubanshe, 2013).
29. *Fuyin de xile* 福音的喜乐 (The Joy of the Gospel) (Macau: Leren chubanshe, 2015).
30. Posted on August 27, 2020.

31. Chen Jianming. "Modern Chinese Attitudes toward the Bible," in *Reading Christian Scriptures in China*, ed. Chloë Starr (London, New York: T & T Clark, 2008), p. 13.
32. See Andy Cheung, "Functionalism and Foreignisation: Applying Skopos Theory to Bible Translation," Ph.D. diss., University of Birmingham, 2011.
33. Ibid., p. 130.
34. Carlo Buzzetti, *La Parola tradotta. Aspetti linguistici, ermeneutici e teologici della Traduzione della Sacra Scrittura* (The Word in Translation. Linguistic, Hermeneutical and Theological Aspects of the Translation of the Sacred Scriptures) (Brescia: Morcelliana, 1973), p. 264. Author's translation.
35. An-Ting Yi, "When Notes Start to Speak: An Investigation of Footnotes and Interlinear Notes in Contemporary Chinese Bible Versions," in *The Bible Translator*, Vol. 69, No. 1 (2018), pp. 56–78.
36. Ibid., p. 75. On other paratextual studies and the *skopos* theory, see Ibid., pp. 57–60; Cheung, "Functionalism and Foreignisation."
37. MS VI C, 30/6 "S. Scrittura, criteri di traduzione. Appunti" (Sacred Scriptures, Criteria of Translation. Notes), Bagheria, PA, September 30, 1960, p. 1. Author's translation.
38. MS XIV, 6, "Pensieri sullo Studio Biblico Cinese" (Thoughts on the Chinese Studium Biblicum), July 11, 1959–July 2, 1960, p. 9. Author's translation.
39. George Kam Wah Mak, "To Add or not to Add? The British and Foreign Bible Society's Defence of the 'Without Note or Comment' Principle in Late Qing China," in *Journal of the Royal Asiatic Society*, Vol. 25 No. 2 (2015), pp. 329–354, 330, 348.

CHAPTER 4

The Use and Reception of the Studium Biblicum Version (*Sigao Shengjing*) by Catholic Communities in China

Monica Romano

Abstract The year 2018 marked the 50th anniversary of the first ever complete Chinese Catholic Bible translation from the original texts in vernacular language, produced by the Studium Biblicum Franciscanum of Hong Kong, under the leadership of the Italian Father Gabriele Maria Allegra, OFM. Known in Chinese as *Sigao Shengjing* 思高圣经, the Studium Biblicum Version remains the most reputable and widely used translation among the Chinese Catholics. This chapter presents the results of a survey conducted among Chinese Catholics living in mainland China. It aimed to understand better Chinese Catholics' use of and views on some of the main contemporary Bible translations, with a special focus on the Studium Biblicum Version.

M. Romano (✉)
Ethnology and Ethno-Anthropology, Sapienza University of Rome, Rome, Italy

51

Keywords Chinese Bible translation · Studium Biblicum translation · *Sigao* Bible · Catholic Church in China · Christianity in China

INTRODUCTION

The Catholic Church in China had to wait until the end of the twentieth century to have a complete translation of the Bible in the Chinese language. Although Protestant Western missionaries had already fully translated the Bible into classical Chinese (*wenyan* 文言) as early as the 1820s, the first complete Chinese Catholic Bible was not published until the 1960s (in separate volumes in 1961 and in a more user-friendly single-volume edition in 1968) by the Studium Biblicum Franciscanum 思高圣经学会 of Hong Kong. The translation work was initiated and led by the Italian Franciscan Father Gabriele Maria Allegra (雷永明, 1907–1976), who was beatified by Pope Benedict XVI in 2012. This Bible edition, known as the Studium Biblicum Version, or in Chinese *Sigao Shengjing* 思高圣经, or the Studium Biblicum Version,[1] was translated into the vernacular from the original texts.[2] Catholic missionaries present in China during the Ming Dynasty (1368–1644) had dedicated themselves to producing other written works to announce the Gospel, mostly of a liturgical, catechetical, or pastoral nature, but had never translated the Bible as a whole. Traditionally, the Catholic Church did not encourage Bible translation and promoted the use of the Latin *Vulgate* during liturgical celebrations, until around the time of the Second Vatican Council (1962–1965).

Later biblical translation efforts by Catholic Western missionaries and Chinese converts, which remained unpublished until the end of the nineteenth century, were largely based on the Latin *Vulgate* and generally only covered the Gospels or the New Testament. After the publication of the Studium Biblicum Version, other Catholic translations were produced over time, some of which are also relatively well known and even in use. These include the Sheshan 佘山 New Testament translation, or the *Yelusaleng Shengjing* 耶路撒冷圣经,[3] by Bishop Aloysius Jin Luxian, S. J. 金鲁贤 (1916–2013) of Shanghai (1994; revised 2004), and the Pastoral Bible or *Muling Shengjing* 牧灵圣经 (published in 1998 in Hong Kong and printed in mainland China in 2000).[4]

This chapter presents the findings of a consultation carried out through an online survey disseminated among Chinese Catholic communities (e.g., laypeople, priests, seminarians, and sisters) from various dioceses in mainland China. This survey sought to collect feedback about Bible access and use, users' preferences regarding the various available Bible translations, readers' reception and understanding of certain biblical passages and terms, and Catholics' views on and expectations of Bible translation for the future. To the best of the author's knowledge, this particular angle of analysis—namely, exploring the perspectives of contemporary Chinese Bible users and readers—represents an innovative contribution to the study of the Bible in China. In fact, although there has been increasing academic interest in studying the Bible in the Chinese context, research has mostly been focused on historical Bible translation and interpretation, or on comparative analyses of different Bible versions. There have been only limited investigations of the reception of the Bible by ordinary contemporary Chinese Bible users, the majority of whom belong to Christian communities.

According to Meng Zhenhua 孟振华 of Nanjing University, who carried out a survey on Bible understanding among the general public in China,[5] "an academic survey of the readers' understanding and reception of the Bible is significant not only in the context of biblical and religious studies, but also in the study of cultural communication. As such, this topic has aroused considerable academic interest."[6] However, Meng also indicates that "many academics focus on historical Chinese biblical readings and interpretations," with investigations of the understanding and reception of the Bible among the Chinese covering a wide timespan (from the sixteenth to the twenty-first centuries) but generally not focusing on the contemporary situation, and that the Chinese "readers" of interest are "usually limited to certain groups or individuals (largely intellectuals with some religious background)."[7] In other words, "the reactions of ordinary readers have often been ignored," and their attitudes toward the Bible require further investigation.[8] Furthermore, Meng notes that "only a few studies, in their fieldwork and surveys, put forth questions directly regarding the biblical text."[9]

In regard to methodology, an online survey development tool was used to share the questions and collect the answers. The questions and answers were in Chinese and the survey was shared through the support of local contacts and, to a lesser extent, through social media channels (i.e., Christian websites, blogs, and Sina Weibo 新浪微博). The survey neither attempted nor claimed statistical relevance, but rather aimed to collect feedback from a wider audience than could have been possible solely through individual interviews. Additionally, it was articulated in such a way that questions and replies were structured around a well-defined framework that would allow for a comparable analysis of the collected individual information, while ensuring that the respondents could express their views comfortably as their identity would not be disclosed and outcomes would be presented in an aggregated manner. The use of online software aimed to minimize inaccuracies in data collection and analysis. There were, however, limitations in the survey. First, the survey was not able to reach a diverse audience (e.g., in terms of education level and age group), possibly due to the fact that not all people were familiar with this type of online tool. Second, the number of respondents varied across sub-categories, particularly among age groups and between laypeople and priests, sisters, and seminarians,[10] making comparisons among them and related outcomes more difficult. Nonetheless, the author believes and hopes that the information collected is insightful and complements the information that has been collected over time on this subject through individual or focus group discussions.

The original survey was broad in focus and audience, targeting Chinese Catholic and Protestant believers living in both China and Italy, but this chapter focuses on the responses from Catholics living in mainland China. The specific objective of this chapter is to draw on the survey responses to provide an overview of the use, reception, and acceptance of the Studium Biblicum Version, which celebrated its fiftieth anniversary in 2018 and has been in use in mainland China for nearly 30 years. The chapter also elaborates on Catholic respondents' views on the Studium Biblicum Version both in its own right and also in comparison with other contemporary Bible translations.[11]

PROFILE OF THE RESPONDENTS

Table 4.1 provides an overview of the profile of the Catholic respondents considered in this chapter.[12]

Most of the Catholic respondents (62%) had been baptized at birth, followed by those who had been baptized for over 15 years (nearly 15%). In regard to education level, 68% were university graduates, with some having obtained postgraduate qualifications. Although most of the respondents (54%) indicated that they had never studied or had formal

Table 4.1 Profile of Chinese Catholic respondents from Mainland China[13]

Number	289[a]
Gender	55% M, 45% F
Age	18–24 (18%), 25–30 (25%), 31–40 (32%), 41–50 (19%), 51+ (5.5%)
Priests, theology seminarians or students, and sisters/novices	35%
Education	Up to junior middle school (16%), high school (14%), university (55%), postgraduate (13%), other (2%)
Residence	56% urban, 44% rural
Baptized	99%

[a]The total number of Catholic respondents from mainland China was 289, but not all of them responded to each question. Some questions were optional, some were targeted to a specific subcategory of respondents (e.g., laypeople, or clergy and religious people including priests, sisters, and seminarians), and some were follow-up questions that depended on previous replies. An initial and substantive question to be responded to was whether the respondent had a Bible at home. Replying "yes" to this question was a pre-requisite for continuing the survey. As two respondents replied negatively to this question, the number of actual respondents was reduced to 287. The total number of respondents who answered all required questions was 246.

training in Christian, theological, or biblical studies, 32.5% had studied theology, 23.5% canon law, 22% the history of Christianity, 19% Christian ethics, and 17% the Bible.[14] The situation was considerably different when looking at the data related to priests and seminarians: over 90% and 80%, respectively, indicated that they had studied theology, and over 60% of both groups had received training in canon law, Christian ethics, or the history of Christianity. A background in biblical studies was less prevalent, being reported by 56% of the priests and 37% of the seminarians. The data related to sisters indicate that they had less training: 58% reported having undertaken theological studies, 19% had studied canon law, 19% Christian ethics, 16% the history of Christianity, and less than 13% the Bible. Nearly a quarter of the sisters had not had an opportunity to undertake such training. Of the respondents who had received training, 59% indicated that they had been trained in churches, followed by Chinese seminaries (23.5%) and Chinese universities (10%). Some of the respondents indicated that they had studied these topics in universities or seminaries in Italy or abroad, and a few explained that they had studied on their own at home or using online resources.

In regard to employment status (excluding priests, sisters, and seminarians), 23% of the lay respondents indicated that they were working in a Chinese company and 12% that they were students, followed by housewives (over 5%), businessmen (nearly 5%), and employees of foreign companies (nearly 5%). Some 3.5% of the respondents were public officials, another 3.5% were unemployed, and over 11% were doing other jobs (e.g., as teachers, owners of shops or private businesses, nurses, social or NGO workers, engineers, and lawyers) or were retired.

The respondents indicated they were originally from different parts of China. Nearly 37% were from Hebei (not including Beijing) and 28% from other provinces.[15] Others were from Liaoning (9%), Shanxi (5.5%), Hubei (5%), and Shaanxi (3.5%). The respondents from Beijing and Shanghai accounted for 6 and 7% of the total, respectively. The respondents' places of residence included Shijiazhuang (16%), Beijing (9%), Shenyang (8%), Shanghai (7%), and Xi'an (3%).[16]

BIBLE PRINTING AND DISTRIBUTION

In mainland China, Bible printing and distribution is subject to strict government regulations in terms of the number of copies that can be printed and the location of distribution and sale. The Bible cannot be sold in ordinary bookstores and is only available in government-sanctioned church bookstores and distribution points. Furthermore, only a few authorized printing houses associated with official churches are permitted to print Bibles for distribution by registered church networks. The largest printing facility is the Nanjing-based Amity Printing Company (*Aide yinshua youxian gongsi* 爱德印刷有限公司), a joint venture owned by the United Bible Societies (UBS) and the Amity Foundation, the latter being a faith-based social development and charity organization associated with the Protestant Three-Self Patriotic Movement (*Sanzi Aiguo Yundong* 三自爱国运动, hereafter the TSPM) and the China Christian Council (*Zhongguo Jidujiao Xiehui* 中国基督教协会). Amity prints Bibles based on printing quotas received annually by the TSPM; however, rather than distributing them directly, it uses a network of 77 distribution points across China.[17] Amity has also printed some copies of the Studium Biblicum Version and the Pastoral Bible. There are three publishing houses affiliated with the Catholic Church: Guangqi Press (*Guangqishe* 光启社) in Shanghai, Hebei Faith Press (*Xindeshe* 信德社) in Shijiazhuang (Hebei), and Sapientia Press (*Shangzhi bianyiguan* 上智编译馆) in Beijing. A number of Bible translations are now also available online and through mobile phone applications, which may have expanded access to the Bible for Chinese readers.

Concerning data on the number of Bibles distributed in China, as of November 2019, Amity Press had printed 85.48 million copies for distribution in the country.[18] Regarding Catholic editions in particular, 4.5 million copies of various Catholic editions of the Bible were printed in mainland China from the 1980s to 2018, of which 2.6 million were copies of the Studium Biblicum Version, which started to be used in the country in the early 1990s.[19] The remaining Catholic Versions that were also printed in this period include a New Testament translation by a Jesuit father from North China—Joseph Hsiao Ching-shan (Xiao Jingshan) 蕭 靜山 (1855–1924)[20]—the Sheshan New Testament Version and Psalms, and the Pastoral Bible.[21]

Although there are a great variety of Protestant Bible editions, encompassing those with different-sized characters (including larger-print versions for the elderly), editions with fashionable covers for younger readers, and parallel and bilingual editions, there is a more limited range of Catholic editions. However, over the past 15 years, efforts have been made to publish different Catholic editions to promote the reading and study of the Bible. The Studium Biblicum Version was published for the first time in mainland China in August 1992, printed with old-style vertical typesetting. An edition with horizontal typesetting was first printed in 2007.[22] In 2009, the UBS and the Taizé Community co-sponsored the printing of one million copies of the Studium Biblicum Version (200,000 complete versions and 800,000 copies of the New Testament, Psalms, and Ecclesiasticus) in a horizontal format by Amity Press.[23]

In May 2014, a bilingual Chinese–English New Testament edition (*Zhongying duizhao* 中英对照), printed horizontally, was published by Faith Press. It consisted of the Studium Biblicum Version and the New American Bible. Claretian Publications and the Pastoral Bible Foundation have also been active in Chinese Bible translation and dissemination work. In addition to the Pastoral Bible, they produce the *Lectio Divina* New Testament (*Xiezhu Dujing—Xinyue* 偕主读经——新约), which was first published in mainland China by Faith Press.[24] The *Lectio Divina* edition complements the biblical text with background explanations and introductions, commentaries, parallel biblical references, and guidelines for the *Lectio Divina*; the New Testament version contained therein is a new translation that is currently being revised, whereas the translation of the Old Testament is still in progress.[25]

On the fiftieth anniversary of the publication of the Studium Biblicum Version in October 2018, a special edition of this translation was published by the Bishops' Conference of the Catholic Church in China, which involved printing 5,000 copies through Amity Press.[26] In 2012, the first ever Chinese–Italian bilingual edition of the New Testament and the Psalms was published in Italy, co-sponsored by the association Piccola Famiglia dell'Assunta, the non-profit charity organization TherAsia, and the Italian priest Father Giuseppe Bellia.[27] The Chinese version was based on the Studium Biblicum Version. Amity Press printed 10,000 copies for free distribution among Chinese Catholics living in Italy.

BIBLE READING AND STUDY

When asked how they had obtained their Bible, over 79% of the Catholic respondents indicated that they had purchased their Bible in church and 23% had received it as a gift.[28] A few of the respondents had bought their Bible in bookstores, used e-versions, or purchased the Bible online.

In regard to the frequency of Bible reading, over 43% of the respondents read the Bible every day and 21% two or three times a week. The frequency was considerably higher among the priests, sisters, and seminarians, over 81% of whom indicated that they read the Bible on a daily basis. Of all of the respondents, 21.5% indicated that they did not read the Bible every week (with this figure less than 9% among the priests, sisters, and seminarians) and some 7% that they read it only on Sundays. A few people noted that their behavior may depend on circumstances, such as work commitments (Fig. 4.1).

Disaggregating the data by age range, it is noticeable that the younger respondents read the Bible less frequently than those in the older age groups. For example, only 14% of the respondents aged 18–24 read the Bible on a daily basis, compared to 60% of those aged 31–40 and 41–50. Among the oldest respondents (aged 51 and over), 36% read the Bible every day. The respondents indicating that they read the Bible two to three times a week declined from over 26.5% of those aged 18–24 to 13% of those aged 31–40, and then increased again among those aged 41–50 and peaked among the oldest respondents (36%). The number of people that do not read the Bible every week also declined with age, from 33% of

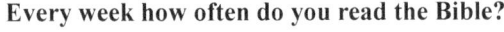

Every week how often do you read the Bible?

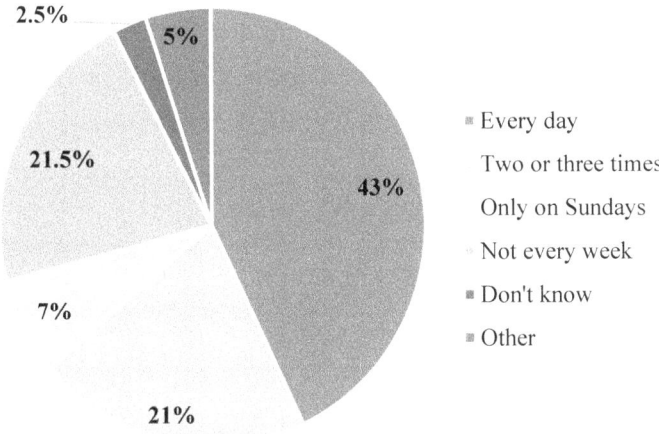

- Every day
- Two or three times
- Only on Sundays
- Not every week
- Don't know
- Other

Fig. 4.1 Frequency of Bible reading

the respondents aged 18–24 to 7% of the respondents aged 51 and over (Fig. 4.2).

Of the respondents, 44% indicated that they had attended Bible training in the past and 26% were attending one at the time of the survey.[29] Fewer respondents noted that they had not planned or did not plan to attend any training, due to a lack of time, opportunity, or interest (see Fig. 4.3). In comparison, the proportion of the Protestant respondents who stated that they often attended Bible training was more than double that of the Catholic respondents, and 37% of the Protestant respondents were attending such training at the time of the survey. However, 28% of the Protestant respondents had attended Bible training in the past, compared to 44.5% of the Catholic respondents. On non-attendance of Bible training, a smaller proportion of Protestants reported not attending Bible training than Catholics, with 3.5% of the former responding that they did not have the time and 4% that there was no class available.

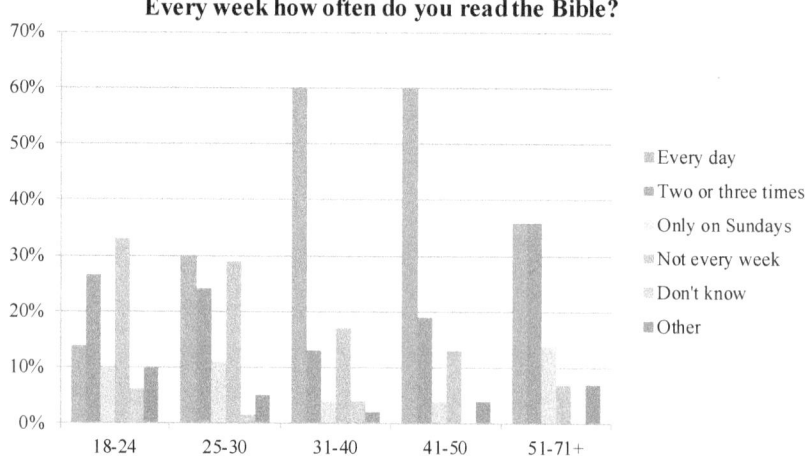

Fig. 4.2   Frequency of Bible reading by age group

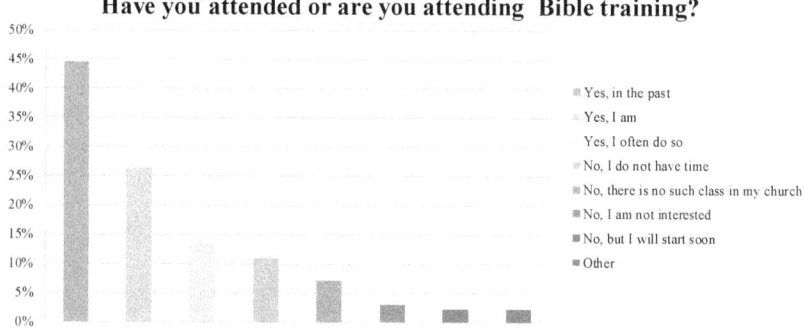

Fig. 4.3   Attendance at Bible training

OWNERSHIP, USE, AND PREFERENCE OF BIBLE EDITIONS

Almost all of the Catholic respondents (99%) indicated that they had a Bible at home, with the exception of two laypeople. One in three Catholics had two Bible editions, nearly one in four had one edition only, and nearly one in five had three editions. The Protestant respondents had a higher number of different editions than the Catholic respondents (Fig. 4.4).

The two younger groups of people owned fewer Bibles than those aged 31 or over. For example, 31% of the respondents aged 18–24 and 29% of those aged 25–30 had only one Bible edition. This figure was lower among the respondents of older age groups, particularly those aged 41–50 (16%). The data were slightly more homogenous across age groups regarding ownership of three Bible editions. Ownership of five or more Bible editions was much higher among the older respondents. For example, more than three times as many of the respondents aged 41–50 owned five Bible editions than of those aged 18–24 (7% of the former versus less than 2% of the latter). Similarly, ownership of more than five Bible editions was more than twice as common among the respondents aged 25–30 and nearly three times as common among the respondents aged 31–40 when compared to those aged 18–24 (4%), with the gap widening further in the two upper age groups (Fig. 4.5).

Among the clergy and religious people, the highest proportion indicated that they had two Bible editions, with considerably fewer owning three or more. Nonetheless, the priests, sisters, and seminarians tended to

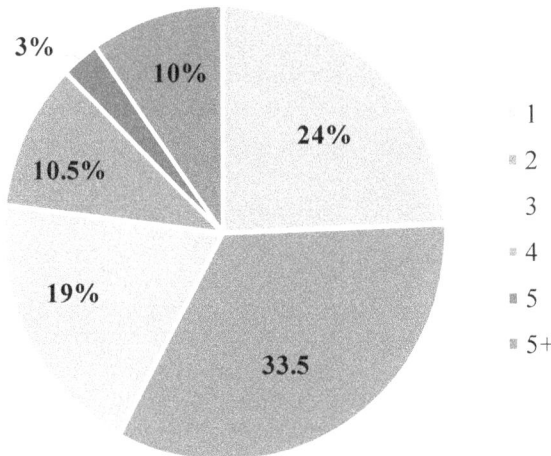

How many Bible editions do you have?

Fig. 4.4 Number of Bible editions owned

How many Bible editions do you have?

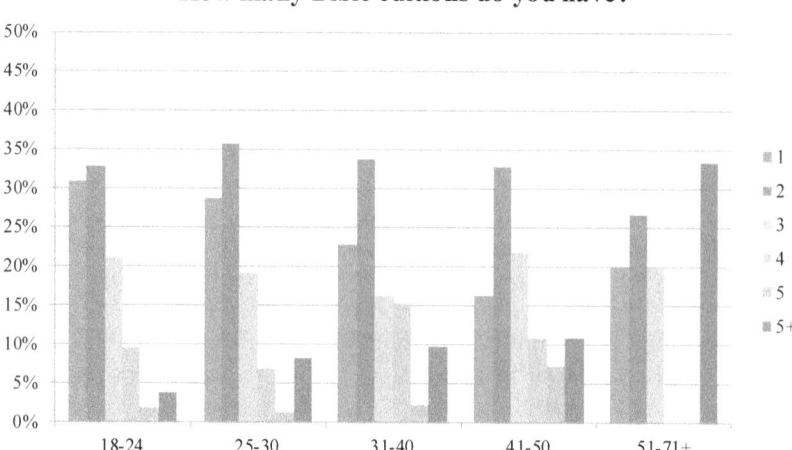

Fig. 4.5   Number of Bible editions owned (by age group)

have a higher number of Bibles overall compared to the laypeople: 17% of the clergy and religious people reported having four editions, compared to 7% of the laypeople, whereas 12% of the former had over five Bibles, compared to 9% of the latter (Fig. 4.6).

Concerning Bible format or type,[30] 93% of the Catholic respondents indicated having a complete edition of the Bible, whereas over a fifth had a bilingual Chinese–English edition and the same fraction had the New Testament only. A few of the respondents added through open comments that they had the Chinese–Italian bilingual version. By comparison, 42% of the Protestant respondents indicated owning a bilingual Chinese–English version, but only 10% of them had the New Testament only (Fig. 4.7).

More than 90% of the respondents across all age groups had a complete Bible, which increased to 96% for the respondents aged 41–50; all of the oldest respondents had at least one copy. The proportion of respondents who owned an edition of the New Testament was in the range of 20–30% for most age groups, including a quarter of the youngest age group and about a fifth of the respondents in the 25–30 and 31–40 age brackets. For the Gospels, 18% and 25% of the respondents aged 41–50 and 51–70+,

How many Bible editions do you have?

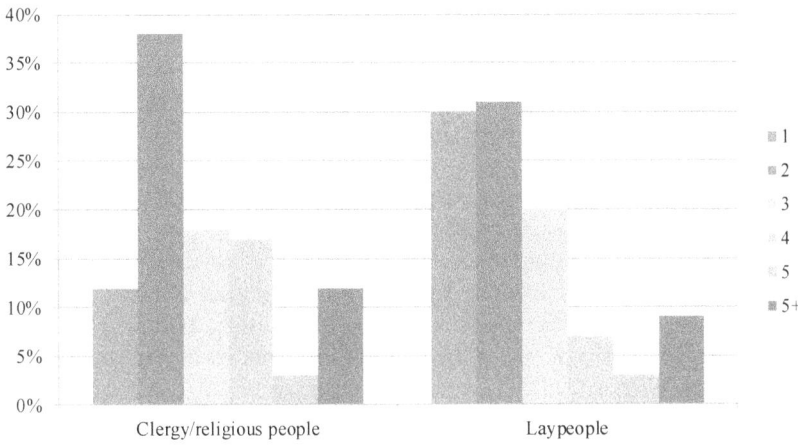

Fig. 4.6 Number of Bible editions owned (clergy/religious people vs. laypeople)

Which Bible format do you have?

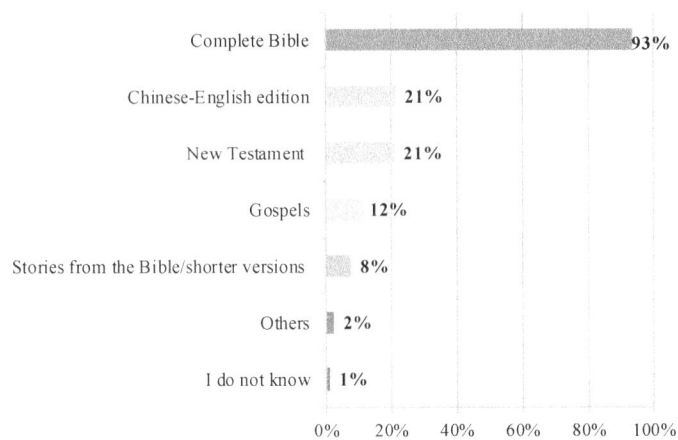

Fig. 4.7 Bible format/type owned

respectively, indicated having an edition; these were the highest proportions across the age groups. Interestingly, several respondents indicated having bilingual Chinese–English Bible editions: 29% of the 41–50 age group, 22% of the 25–30 age group, and 20% of the 31–40 age group.

No significant differences emerged between the clergy/religious people and the laypeople, with the exception of 28% of the former having a Chinese–English edition, compared to only 18% of the latter. Well above 90% of both categories had a complete Bible edition (96% of the priests, sisters, and seminarians and 92% of the laypeople).

On the specific Bible translation(s) owned,[31] 88% of the Catholic respondents indicated owning the Studium Biblicum Version, with the second most popular being the Pastoral Bible (40%). It is worth noting that over one-fifth of the Catholic respondents also had the Union Version, or *Heheben* 和合本, which is the most popular and widespread Bible translation among Protestant Chinese.[32] It is also likely that this understates the actual number of respondents with a copy of the Union Version, as some referred in their open comments to "the Protestant translation" or "the Protestant Bible" (which is likely to indicate the Union Version) or to the "Chinese–English bilingual version," which could also be a bilingual Chinese–English Protestant edition in which the Chinese translation is that of the Union Version. Some 18% of the respondents indicated having the Sheshan New Testament version. Of these, 15% were from Shanghai or were living in the city at the time of the survey. Additionally, the respondents having the Sheshan New Testament edition accounted for 40% of the total respondents that were originally from Shanghai and 38% of those residing there. Interestingly, however, 25% of the respondents from Hebei and 19% of those living in Beijing also indicated that they had the Sheshan edition. Unlike the Protestant respondents, only a minority of the Catholic respondents indicated that they had the Today's Chinese Version (*Xiandai Zhongwen Yiben* 现代中文译本)[33] (Fig. 4.8).

The data also show a significant gap between the male and female respondents. For example, 92% of the male respondents indicated that they had the Studium Biblicum Version, compared to 84% of the female respondents. The gap is also significant in relation to other Bible translations, such as the Pastoral Bible (45% versus 35% for men and women,

Which Bible translation do you have?

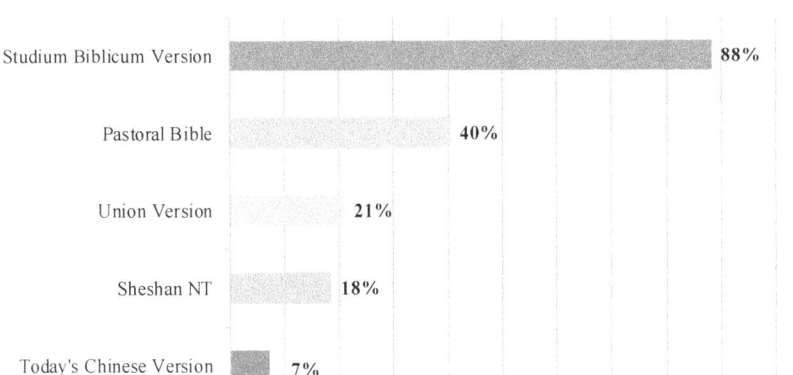

Fig. 4.8 Bible translations owned

respectively), the Union Version (31% versus 9%), and the Sheshan version (24% versus 11.5%)

Disaggregated by different age groups, the data confirm that (the Studium Biblicum Version) remained the most widespread edition among Catholics regardless of age, with even the lowest percentage being above 80%. However, the proportion of respondents indicating that they had this edition increased with age, with the highest percentage found among those aged 41–50 (96%). A similar trend can be observed in relation to the Pastoral Bible. The highest proportion of respondents having the Union Version and the Sheshan New Testament were in the 31–40 age group, at 28% and 25%, respectively (Fig. 4.9).

The priests, sisters, and seminarians tended to have a higher number of Bible translations than the laypeople. A large majority of the former indicated that they had the Studium Biblicum Version—15% more than the laypeople and 10% more than the overall sample. Similarly, the percentage of the former owning the Pastoral Bible was nearly double that of laypeople, and nearly 40% had the Sheshan version, which was four times higher than the proportion of laypeople (Fig. 4.10).

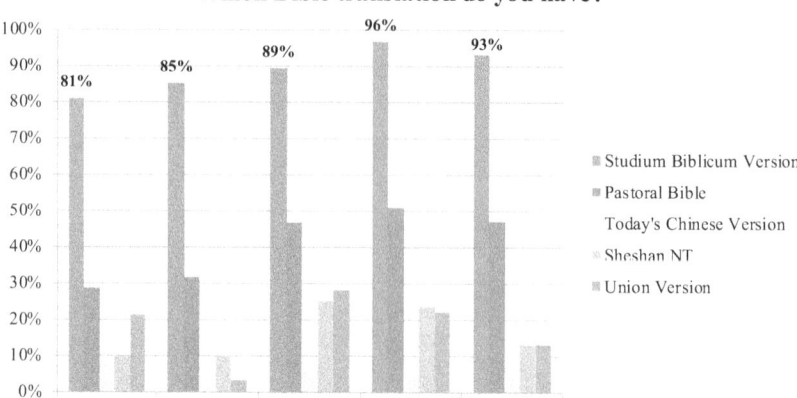

Fig. 4.9   Bible translations owned by age group

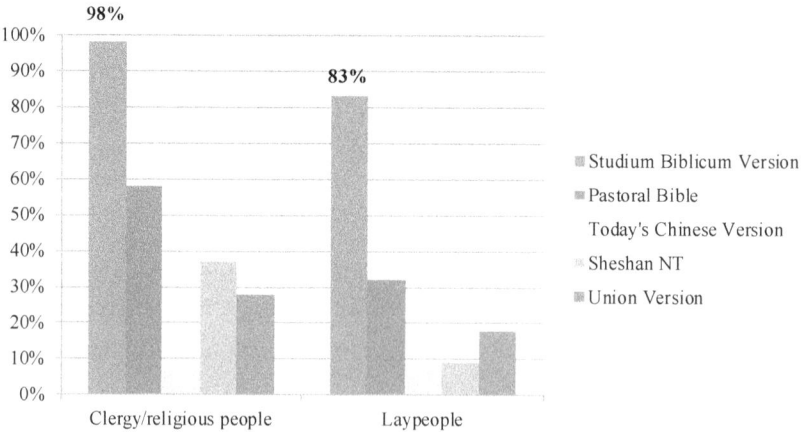

Fig. 4.10   Bible translations owned (clergy/religious vs. laypeople)

A large majority of the respondents (85%) indicated that they generally used the Studium Biblicum Version, but this percentage is slightly less than those indicating to own such Bible version (88%).[34] Additionally, compared to data related to ownership, there was a wider gap between this and other Bible editions (Fig. 4.11).

Disaggregated by age group, the trends were similar to those related to ownership of the Bible: the Studium Biblicum Version tended to be used less by the younger respondents and more by the older respondents. Significant gaps were notable between the youngest respondents (77% of whom used the Studium Biblicum Version) and other age groups, with a difference of 5% for the respondents aged 25–30 and of 16% for the respondents aged 41–50 (Fig. 4.12).

Comparing the responses of the priests, sisters, and seminarians with those of the laypeople, the former tended to use the Studium Biblicum Version more than the latter, although in both cases the figures were lower than those related to ownership (Fig. 4.13).

Figure 4.14 provides an overview of the responses related to the use of the Studium Biblicum Version by certain categories of respondents. Notably, there was a wide gap between the male and female respondents, with 90% of men using this edition versus 78% of women; also, 95% of the religious people used the Studium Biblicum Version versus 79% of the laypeople.

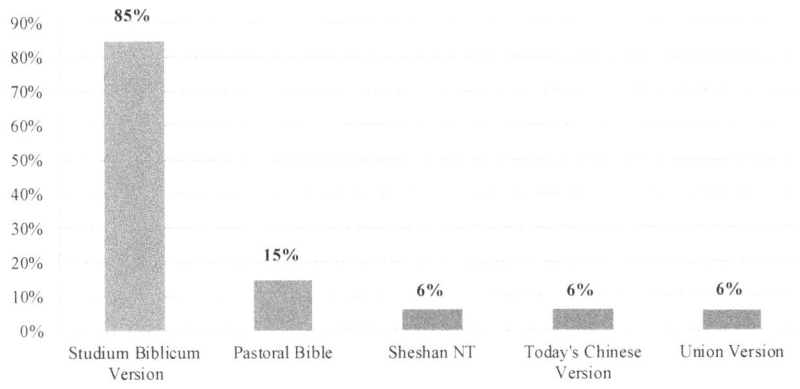

Which Bible translation do you generally use?

Fig. 4.11 Bible translations generally used

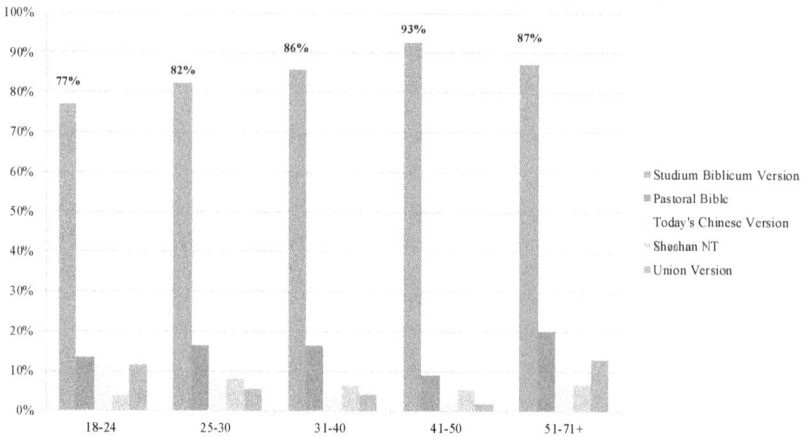

Fig. 4.12   Bible translations generally used by age group

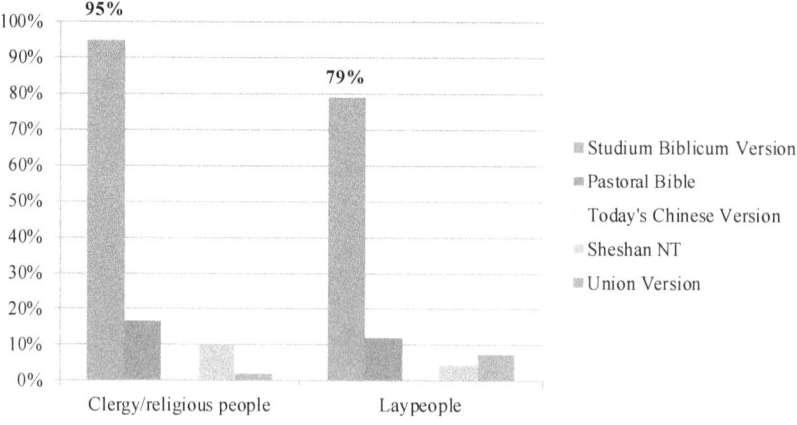

Fig. 4.13   Bible translations generally used (clergy/religious vs. laypeople)

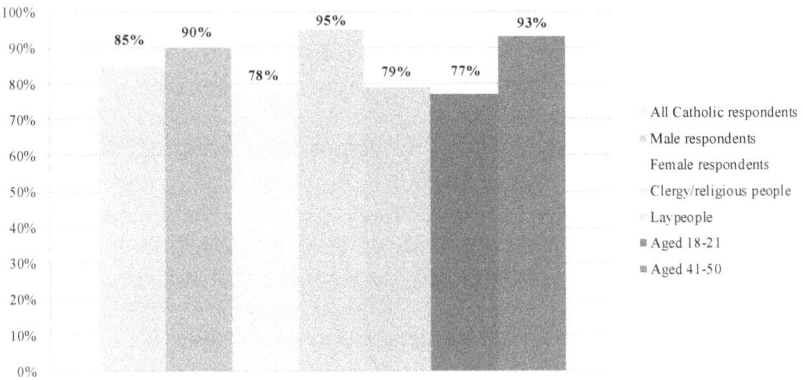

Fig. 4.14 Respondents Generally Using the Studium Biblicum Version

When asked to indicate which Bible edition they used the most,[35] the majority of the respondents chose the Studium Biblicum Version, with the use of other editions negligible (Fig. 4.15).

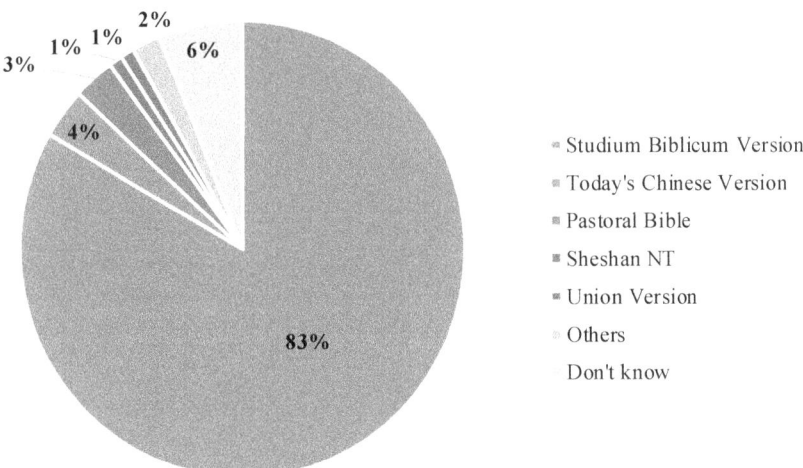

Fig. 4.15 Most used Bible translation

The survey confirmed that the Studium Biblicum Version was also the most used Bible edition in the context of Mass and community activities in the church, such as training sessions, spiritual retreats, and Bible classes.[36] No other translation scored even 10% of responses apart from the Pastoral Bible, which 15% of the respondents indicated was used for some group activities (Fig. 4.16).

The survey also asked the respondents to indicate their preferred translations.[37] Over 80% of the respondents opted for the Studium Biblicum Version, and there was a huge gap between the first preference and the second (Fig. 4.17).

With similar trends to those related to ownership and use, the younger respondents expressed a lower preference for the Studium Biblicum Version compared to those in the 31–50 age group. However, the oldest respondents also expressed a lower preference for this translation (Fig. 4.18).

The responses to this question also reveal a large gap between the preferences indicated by the priests, sisters, and seminarians and those of the laypeople. Nearly all of the former expressed a preference for the Studium Biblicum Version, representing a 20% higher proportion than that among the laypeople (Fig. 4.19).

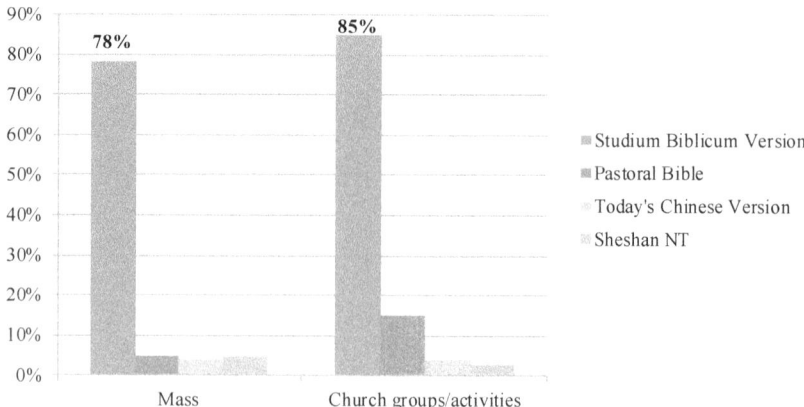

Which Bible translations are mostly used for Mass and church/group activities?

Fig. 4.16   Bible translations used for Mass and church activities

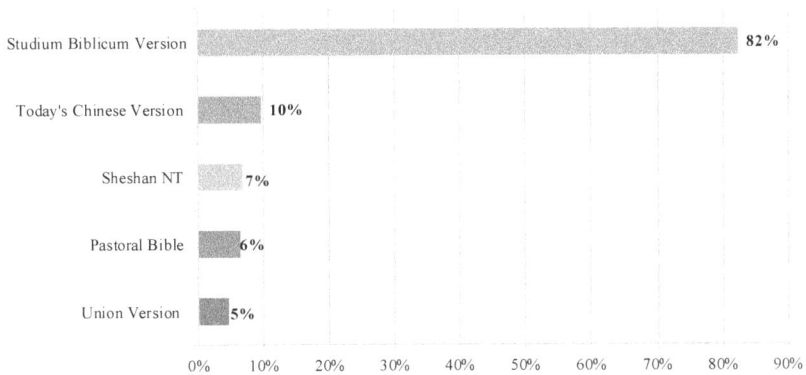

Fig. 4.17   Preferred Bible translations

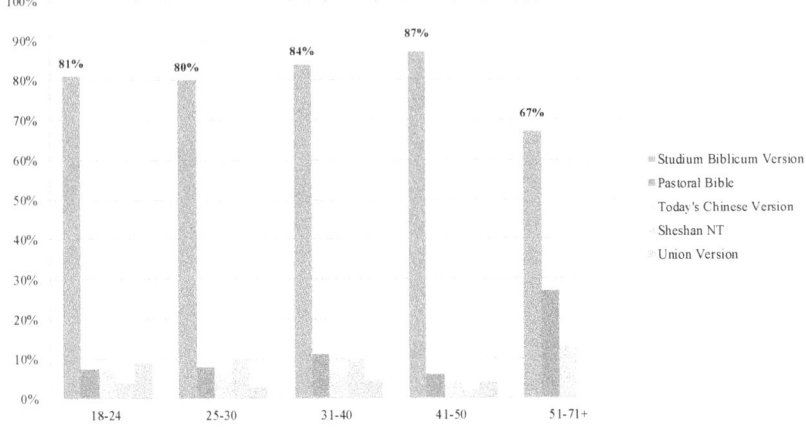

Fig. 4.18   Preferred Bible translations by age group

When preferences for the Studium Biblicum Version were specifically analyzed based on the responses of different group categories, it is noteworthy that the highest preference was expressed by the male respondents

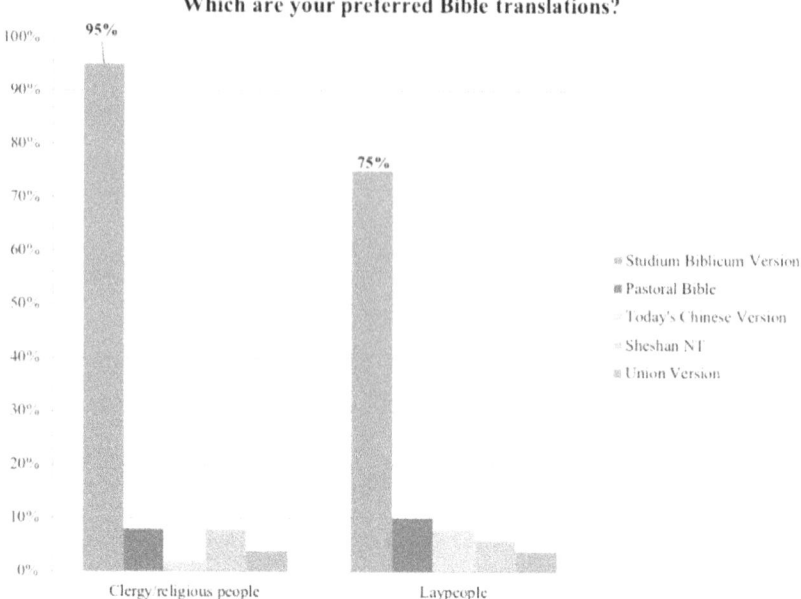

Fig. 4.19   Preferred Bible translations (clergy/religious vs. laypeople)

(13 percentage points higher than among the female respondents) and—as noted above—by the priests, seminarians, and sisters compared to all of the respondents and the laypeople (Fig. 4.20).

Some of the respondents explained why the Studium Biblicum Version was their preferred translation. Most believed this translation to be authoritative, accurate, and reliable, as it is based on the original texts, and hence, it is closer to the original biblical meanings. Some of the respondents noted that they were familiar with this translation, that they had always used it, or that it was commonly used in their church community. Others explained that it was the edition officially approved by Church authorities or that it was recommended by their priests. Many expressed appreciation for its elegant style and the beauty of its language. Some indicated that it was convenient for them to use as it adopts the proper names and place names commonly used in church and is complemented with a detailed and useful commentary.

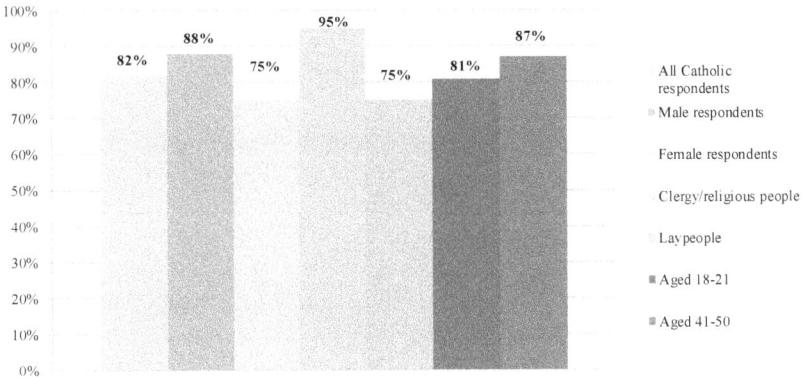

Fig. 4.20 To Respondents Preferring the Studium Biblicum Version

Comparing data related to ownership, use, and preferences of the Studium Biblicum Version, we can conclude that a large majority of the Catholic respondents had this Bible edition at home and were making use of it, including for collective church activities. However, it emerged from the responses that this version was used more for group activities in the church than for Mass (Fig. 4.21).

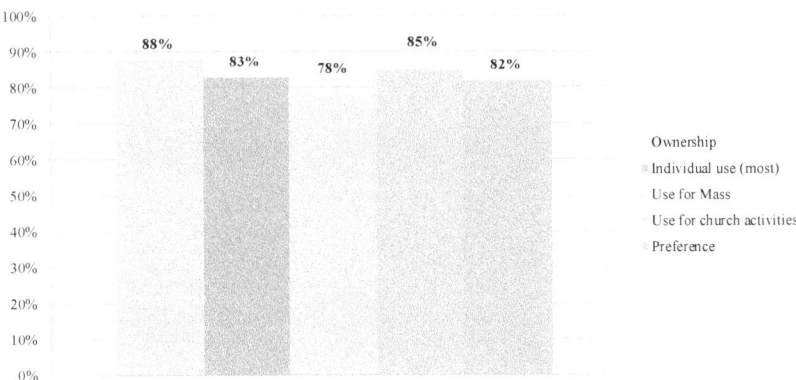

Fig. 4.21 The Studium Biblicum Version: Ownership, Usage, and Preference

PREFERRED TRANSLATION OF BIBLICAL PASSAGES

The majority of the Catholic respondents (61%) stated that the Bible is somewhat difficult to understand (Fig. 4.22).

The survey included a few passages from the New Testament, extracted from some of the most popular contemporary Chinese Bible translations, inviting the respondents to provide feedback on translation preferences and their understanding of meanings.[38]

Concerning a passage in the well-known Prologue of the Gospel according to St. John (Jn 1:14), "And the Word became flesh," 71% of the Catholic respondents expressed a preference for the translation of the Studium Biblicum Version (*shengyan chengle xuerou* 圣言成了血肉). The main issue in this passage remains the translation of the term *logos* ("Word"), which is rendered with the term *shengyan* 圣言, commonly used in the Catholic Church,[39] as opposed to the near unanimous use of the term *dao* 道 among Protestants.[40] Some of the Catholic respondents elaborated on why they believed *shengyan* to be the better translation. They noted that the term *dao* is ambiguous and could be misleading, as it could be associated with Laozi 老子 or Daoism. On the contrary believed that *shengyan* more accurately and faithfully renders the original term *logos*, is clearer, and is now commonly used by the Church. Fewer of the Catholic respondents expressed a preference for *dao*, which

Is the Bible easy/difficult to understand?

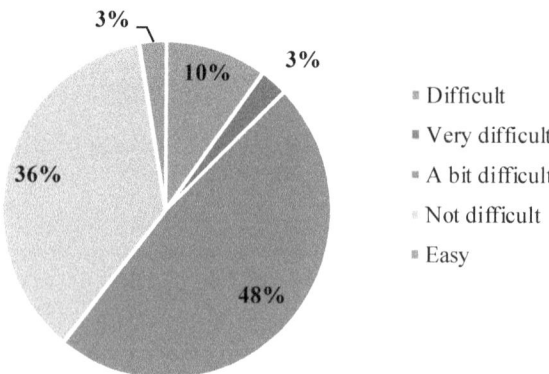

Fig. 4.22   Perceived difficulty of understanding the Bible

would have the advantage of making the translation closer to the Chinese cultural tradition; furthermore, *dao* is a term known to everybody and would be easier to understand.

Another problematic aspect of this passage is how to render the term *sarx* ("flesh" in the English translation given above), as evidenced by the different translations used in various Chinese Bible Versions. The Studium Biblicum Version adopts the term *xuerou* 血肉 (literally "blood and flesh"), but others, such as the Today's Chinese Version and the Pastoral Bible, avoid the literal translation and choose a more straightforward yet not fully accurate rendering with the term *ren* 人 (person or "human being"). The latter translation therefore reads "The Word became a person or human being" rather than "The Word became flesh." Disaggregating the data by group category, 77.5% of the priests, sisters, and seminarians and 67% of the laypeople expressed a preference for the translation of *xuerou* used by the Studium Biblicum Version.

The passage from the Gospel of St. Luke (Lk 4:18), "The Spirit of the Lord is upon me, because he has anointed me...," includes a Semitic expression ("to anoint") that may be difficult to understand for those not familiar with the Jewish cultural background. Nearly 40% of the Catholic respondents opted for the translation in the Studium Biblicum Version (*yinwei ta gei wo chuanle you* 因为他给我傅了油), which renders "anoint" literally with the term *chuanyou* 傅油 ("to spread oil"). Notably, however, nearly one-third of the respondents expressed a preference for the translation in the Today's Chinese Version, which avoids a literal translation and opts for the term *jianxuan* 拣选 ("to choose"), such that the passage reads *yinwei ta jianxuanle wo* 因为他拣选了我 (literally, "because he has chosen me"). Looking at answers provided by the laypeople only, 42% of them opted for this translation, compared to 13% of the priests, sisters, and seminarians. In contrast, a higher percentage of the latter expressed a preference for the translation of the Studium Biblicum Version (59%), compared to 29.5% of the laypeople. A slightly higher percentage of the Protestant than the Catholic respondents expressed a preference for the translation removing the Semitic expression, but a lower percentage of the former chose the translation included in their main Bible edition (i.e., the Union Version), at 10 percentage points less than the Catholic respondents expressing a preference for the Studium Biblicum Version. Finally, it is remarkable that nearly 20% of the respondents preferred the translation in the Sheshan New Testament version (*yinwei ta gei wo fule you* 因为他给我敷了油): 25% of the clergy/religious people and 18% of the laypeople. This version also adopts a literal translation, but uses a different term, *fuyou* 敷油 ("apply ointment").

HOPES AND EXPECTATIONS FOR THE FUTURE

Finally, the survey investigated the views of Catholic believers with respect to the future prospects of Bible translation, inquiring whether they believed there was a need for a new translation or it was suitable to keep using one of the existing versions.

The laypeople were nearly equally split among those willing to use the same Bible edition they had been using and those expressing a desire for a new translation. Only a minority indicated a preference to shift to a different translation already in use (Fig. 4.23).

The female respondents were more inclined to express the need for a new translation: 41.5% of them, compared to 34% of the male respondents, expressed this preference. However, the responses were equally balanced between the men and women with respect to the need to continue to use the same translation (about 42% of both the male and

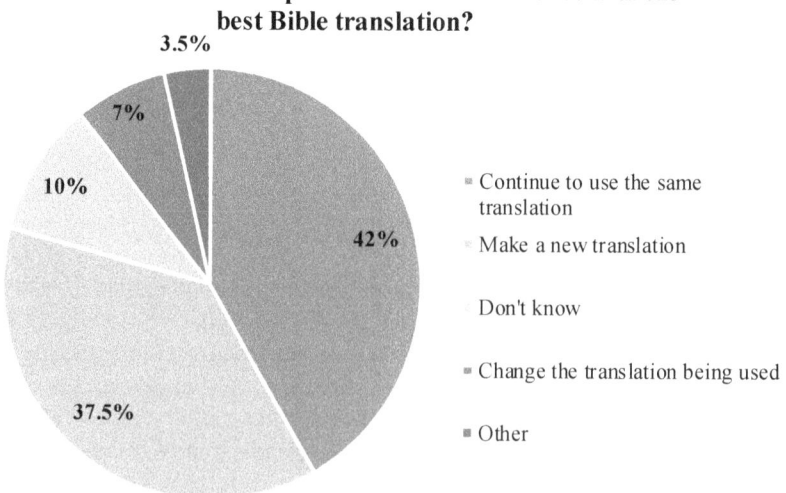

What should be done to provide Chinese Catholics with the best Bible translation?

- Continue to use the same translation
- Make a new translation
- Don't know
- Change the translation being used
- Other

Fig. 4.23 Views on prospects for future Bible translation (laypeople)

female respondents) or to change to another (8% of the male respondents and 6% of the female respondents). Looking at the different age groups, it is notable that the option for a new translation was preferred by nearly one-third of the youngest respondents, one-third of the respondents aged 25–30, and over half of the respondents aged 41–50. Half of the respondents within the 25–30 age group preferred to continue to use the same translation, which is a higher percentage than that of those aged 18–24 and 31–40 (each at 40%), and those aged 41–50 (36%) and 51–71+ (30%).

The same question was asked to the priests, sisters, and seminarians, with an additional they could choose of revising an existing Bible edition. Most preferred this option but, as was the case for the laypeople, there was no strong prevalence, and this category of respondents was equally split between the two main options of undertaking a revision or continuing with the currently used Bible edition (Fig. 4.24).

Similar to the data related to the laypeople, a higher number of the sisters and female religious people expressed the desire for some change: 35% of them opted for pursuing a new translation, compared to only 7.5% of the priests and seminarians. However, 47% of the latter, as opposed to

What should be done to provide Chinese Catholics with the best Bible translation?

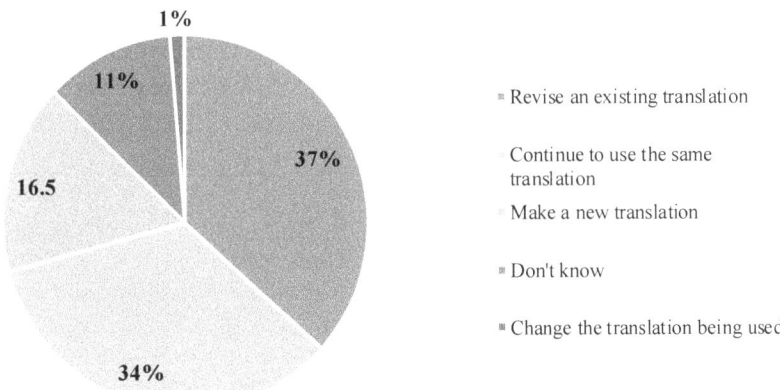

Revise an existing translation

Continue to use the same translation

Make a new translation

Don't know

Change the translation being used

Fig. 4.24 Views on prospects for future Bible translation (clergy/religious people)

15% of the sisters and female religious, wished for a revision of the Bible to be undertaken. Data related to using the same translation were more balanced, with slightly fewer female respondents willing to retain the use of the current translation (31%) compared to the male respondents (36%).

When asked which was the most suitable Bible translation from the pastoral point of view, 77% of the priests, sisters, and seminarians indicated the Studium Biblicum Version. There was, again, a major gap between this and all other translations, with little preference for even the second most preferred option (Fig. 4.25).

Nearly all of the respondents who stated that a Bible revision should be undertaken (97%) indicated that this should be done using the Studium Biblicum translation as a basis.

What is the best translation from the pastoral point of view?

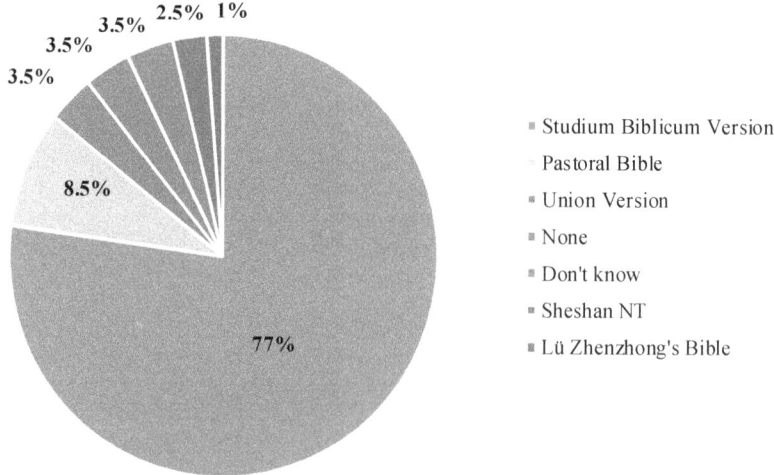

Fig. 4.25   Most suitable Bible from pastoral perspective (clergy/religious people)

Conclusion

Despite a number of new Bible translations having been produced over time, and especially over the past few decades, 50 years after its publication and nearly 30 years after it started to be used in mainland China, the Studium Biblicum Version remains the most widespread and most commonly used translation of the Bible among the Catholic faithful. It is considered authoritative, reputable, and elegant, and none of the other complete or partial Bible translations produced after its publication have thus far been able to challenge its predominance. Nonetheless, over one-third of the Catholic respondents expressed a desire for a new translation or a revision, albeit still based on the Studium Biblicum Version.

Notes

1. In this chapter, this Bible is referred to as the Studium Biblicum Version or the *Sigao* Bible, as it is named in Chinese.
2. For more information about this translation, see Arnulf Camps, OFM, "Father Gabriele M. Allegra, O.F M. (1907–1976) and the Studium Biblicum Franciscanum: The First Complete Chinese Catholic Translation of the Bible," in *Bible in Modern China: The Literary and Intellectual Impact*, eds. Irene Eber, Sze-kar Wan, and Knut Walf, Monumenta Serica Monograph Series XLIII (Sankt Augustin/Nettetal: Steyler Verlag, 1999), pp. 55–76; Thor Strandenaes, *Principles of Chinese Bible Translation, as Expressed in Five Selected Versions of the New Testament and Exemplified by Mt 5:1-12 and Col 1* (Stockholm: Almqvist & Wiksell International, 1987), pp. 100–111.
3. Available only in simplified Chinese, this New Testament edition was published with the title *Shengjing Xinjing Quanji* 圣经新经全集, after the publication of the Gospels in 1986 and subsequently the other New Testament books in separate volumes. It is commonly known as the Sheshan version or the Sheshan edition, taking its name from Sheshan 佘山, a location near Shanghai where the diocesan seminary is sited. In some cases, it is also known as the Chinese "Jerusalem Bible" due to its use of *La Bible de Jérusalem* was used as its textual basis. For more detail on this translation, see Cai Jintu 蔡锦图 (Daniel Kam-to Choi), "Tianzhujiao Zhongwen Shengjing Fanyi de Lishi he Banben" 天主教中文圣经翻译的历史和版本 (The History and Editions of Catholic

Chinese Bible Translations), in *Tianzhujiao Yanjiu Xuebao* 天主教
研究学报 (*Hong Kong Journal of Catholic Studies*), No. 2 (2011),
pp. 38–39; Cai Jintu 蔡锦图 (Daniel Kam-to Choi), *Shengjing
zai Zhongguo—fu Zhongwen Shengjing Lishi Mulu* 圣经在中国—
—附中文圣经历史目录 (The Bible in China: With a Historical
Catalogue of the Chinese Bible) (Hong Kong: Institute of Sino-
Christian Studies, 2018), pp. 87–88; John Baptist Zhang Shijiang,
"The Promotion of the Bible in Contemporary China and Evangelization," *Tripod*, Vol. 27, No. 144 (Spring 2007), http://
hsstudyc.org.hk/en/tripod_en/en_tripod_144_03.html (accessed
January 27, 2021); Monica Romano, "The Sheshan New Testa-
ment Translation by Bishop Jin Luxian of Shanghai," in *Foreign
Missionaries and the Indigenization of the Chinese Catholic Church*,
ed. Cindy Yik-yi Chu (Hong Kong: Centre for Catholic Studies,
The Chinese University of Hong Kong, 2017), pp. 125–170. In
this chapter, this translation is referred to as the Sheshan (New
Testament) translation/edition/version (abbreviated as Sheshan
NT).

4. Cai Jintu, "Tianzhujiao Zhongwen Shengjing Fanyi de Lishi he
Banben," p. 39. The Pastoral Bible was the outcome of the translation efforts of a group of Chinese translators coordinated by the
French Claretian Father Bernard Hurault (于贺, 1924–2004). It is
the Chinese version of the Christian Community Bible, which was
published first in 1988 in the Philippines as the English version of
the popular *Biblia Latinoamericana*. The Pastoral Bible in Chinese
gained some popularity as it reads clearly and smoothly. However,
it has also received some criticism as the biblical and theological
formations of the translators were questioned and some inaccuracies were identified. For more information about this translation,
see Daniel Kam-to Choi and George Kam Wah Mak, "Catholic
Bible Translation in Twentieth-Century China: An Overview,"
in *Catholicism in China, 1900–Present*, ed. Cindy Yik-yi Chu
(New York: Palgrave Macmillan, 2014), pp. 116–117; Cai Jintu,
"Tianzhujiao Zhongwen Shengjing Fanyi de Lishi he Banben,"
pp. 39–40; Cai Jintu, *Shengjing zai Zhongguo*, p. 93. For a compar-
ative analysis of this translation, see Monica Romano, "Issues,
Trends and Cultural Adjustments in Translating the Bible into
Chinese," in *Italian Association for Chinese Studies: Selected Papers*,
Vol. 1, ed. Paola Paderni Venezia (Libreria Editrice Cafoscarina,

2016), pp. 182–206; Monica Romano, "Translating and Transplanting the Word of God in Chinese," in *Sinicising Christianity*, ed. Yangwen Zheng (Leiden: Brill, 2017), pp. 167–194.

5. Zhenhua Meng, "The Understanding of the Bible among the General Public in Mainland China: A Survey on the 'Bullet Curtain' of The Bible," in *Yearbook of Chinese Theology 2015*, Vol. 1, ed. Paulus Huang (Leiden: Brill, 2015), pp. 139–159. This survey focuses not directly on the biblical text, but on analyzing comments made by the Chinese audience (both believers and non-believers) to an American television series about the Bible to "determine how the Chinese read and understand the Bible as well as the reasons behind their behavior."

6. Ibid., p. 139.

7. Ibid., pp. 141–142.

8. Ibid., pp. 142–143.

9. Ibid., p. 143.

10. This category is also referred to in this chapter as clergy/religious people.

11. A paper on the use and reception of the Bible among the Protestant communities in mainland China, with a focus on the Mandarin-language Union Version of the Bible, is currently being finalized. Some insights from this study are reflected in this chapter for comparative purposes but will be presented in full as a separate contribution.

12. The survey was launched online in early 2014 and received 521 responses, of which 318 were from Catholics (289 from mainland China, 26 from Italy, and 3 from other countries), 188 from Protestants (186 from mainland China, one from Italy, and one from other countries), and 15 from non-believers or adherents of other religions (14 from mainland China and one from other countries). The total number of Catholic and Protestant respondents from mainland China was, therefore, 475. Some preliminary results of this survey were included in Romano, "The Sheshan New Testament Translation," pp. 125–170. At that time (August 2015), the survey had received a fewer number ofresponses or a more limited number of responses.

13. Any discrepancy in numbers throughout the figures is due to rounding up or down.

14. Multiple answers were allowed for this question.

15. Mostly Guangdong, Shandong, and Zhejiang and, to a lesser extent, Fujian and Henan, followed by Gansu, Guangxi, Heilongjiang, Jiangsu, Jiangxi, Jilin, Tianjin, with a few respondents from Anhui, Chongqing, Inner Mongolia, and Sichuan.

16. Other cities that were indicated frequently included Chongqing; Fuzhou (Fujian); Lanzhou (Gansu); Guangzhou (Guangdong); Handan, Hengshui, Tangshan, and Xingtai (Hebei); Harbin (Heilongjiang); Zhengzhou (Henan); Wuhan (Hubei); Nanjing (Jiangsu); Nanchang (Jiangxi); Changchun (Jilin); Taiyuan (Shanxi); Hangzhou and Wenzhou (Zhejiang); Qingdao; Shenzhen; and Tianjin.

17. Liu Dong, "The Bible Business," *Global Times*, November 20, 2013, http://www.globaltimes.cn/content/826413.shtml (accessed January 27, 2021).

18. A further 114.5 million copies were printed in more than 130 languages for distribution in 147 countries, for a total of 200 million copies. See "Amity Celebrates its 200 millionth Printed Bible" November 23, 2019, http://www.amityprinting.com/en/gsyw/info.aspx?itemid=245 (accessed January 27, 2021).

19. "Zhongguo Tianzhujiaowang: Jinian Sigao Shengjing Faxing Wushi Zhounian Zuotanhui zai Jing Juxing" 中国天主教网: 纪念思高《圣经》发行五十周年座谈会在京举行, *Xinde.org*, October 24, 2018, https://www.xinde.org/show/43903; "Zhang Shijiang Shenfu zai 'Jinian Sigao Shengjing Chuban 50 Zhounian' Zuotanhuishang de Jianghua" 张士江神父在"纪念思高圣经出版50周年"座谈会上的讲话, *Xinde.org*, October 24, 2018, https://www.xinde.org/show/43909 (accessed January 27, 2021).

20. This New Testament version was published with the title of *Xinjin Quanji* 新经全集; it was translated from the Latin *Vulgate* and its first edition first published in 1922 in Hebei. A revised version was made by other Jesuits in Taiwan and was published in 1956. The 1922 edition was reprinted in the 1980s. Xiao's New Testament edition was of great importance to the life of the Catholic Church in China as it was the most widespread edition, including being used for formation in seminaries, until the Studium Biblicum Version started to be authorized for use in mainland China in the 1990s. For more information on this New Testament translation, see Zhang, "The Promotion of the Bible in Contemporary China

and Evangelization"; Choi and Mak, "Catholic Bible Translation in Twentieth-Century China," pp. 109–115.

21. "Zhongguo Tianzhujiaowang: Jinian Sigao Shengjing Faxing WushiZhounian Zuotanhui zai Jing Juxing."

22. See the preface to *Shengjing. Jinian Sigao Shengjing Chuban 50 Zhounian (1968–2018)* 圣经。纪念思高圣经出版50周年 (1968–2018) (The Holy Bible. In Commemoration of the Fiftieth Anniversary of the Publishing of the Studium Biblicum Version [1968–2018]) (Beijing: Zhongguo Tianzhujiao zhujiaotuan, 2018).

23. "1 million Bibles and New Testament for Catholics in China," *United Bible Societies*, July 30, 2009, https://www.ubscp.org/catholic-bible/ (accessed January 27, 2021).

24. *Xie Zhu Dujing—Xinyue* 偕主读经—新约 (*Lectio Divina*: New Testament) (Shijiazhuang: Faith Press, 2015). The *Lectio Divina* edition was previously published in Macau in 2014 with the title *Xinyue Shengjing Leren Banben fu Zhushi ji Xiezhu Dujing* 新约圣经乐仁译本附注释及偕主读经; Cai Jintu, *Shengjing zai Zhongguo*, pp. 94–96.

25. "New Testament for Mainland China," Macau Bulletin [blog], January 1, 2016, http://macaubulletin.blogspot.com/2016/01/new-testament-for-mainland-china.html (accessed January 27, 2021); "Claretian House in Hong Kong," *Sunday Examiner*, September 1, 2019, http://sundayex.catholic.org.hk/node/562 (accessed January 27, 2021); personal communications from Father Alberto Rossa CMF, Director of Pastoral Bible Foundation, August 2014 and August 2020.

26. *Shengjing. Jinian Sigao Shengjing Chuban 50 Zhounian (1968–2018)*.

27. *Xinyue Shengjing fu Shengyongji—Zhongyi Duizhao* 新约圣经附圣咏集——中意对照 (Nuovo Testamento e Salmi: Cinese–Italiano) (Nanjing: Amity Printing Company, 2012).

28. Multiple answers were allowed.

29. Multiple answers were allowed.

30. Multiple answers were allowed.

31. Multiple answers were allowed.

32. The Union Version was the outcome of a concerted effort made during the nineteenth century and the beginning of the twentieth century by all Protestant denominations in China to translate a

common Bible. Initially produced as "one Bible in three versions" (namely in classical, semi-classical, and Mandarin Chinese), the Mandarin version published in 1919, at the time of the May Fourth Movement, has become very popular and has always been considered as the Chinese Bible par excellence. A revision of the Mandarin Union Version was completed in 2010, following the 1988 publication of an edition with new punctuation. For more information about the Union Version, see Jost Oliver Zetzsche, *The Bible in China: The History of the Union Version or the Culmination of Protestant Missionary Bible Translation in China* (Sankt Augustin: Monumenta Serica Monograph Series XLV, Monumenta Serica Institute, 1999); Strandenaes, *Principles of Chinese Bible Translation*, pp. 76–99. When the Union Version is referred to in this chapter, this means the Mandarin Union Version, unless otherwise specified.

33. The Today's Chinese Version is a Protestant translation published in the 1980s (and revised in 1995) by the United Bible Societies (UBS); it was translated from its English equivalent, the Today's English Version, according to Eugene Nida's principle of "functional equivalence" or "dynamic equivalence," as opposed to "formal correspondence." Whereas the latter focuses on formal fidelity and attempts to reproduce as closely as possible the formal elements of the source text and original language, the principle of functional or dynamic equivalence is to render "in the receptor language the closest natural equivalence of the source-language message," emphasizing the transmission of meaning and content. This translation adopts a clear, simple, and comprehensible language. A Catholic edition of the New Testament was also published, which differs from the Protestant edition only in the terms "God" and "Holy Spirit." These terms are translated according to the consolidated use of the respective communities: *Shangdi*上帝 or *Shen* 神 for "God" and *Shengling* 圣灵 for "Holy Spirit" in the Protestant edition, and *Tianzhu*天主for "God" and *Shengshen* 圣神 for "Holy Spirit" in the Catholic edition. Notably, the Catholic edition retains the term *dao* 道 to translate "Word" (*logos*), as widely used in the Protestant translations, instead of adopting the term *shengyan* 圣言 as used in the Studium Biblicum Version. For more details about the Today's Chinese Version, see Strandenaes, *Principles of Chinese Bible Translation*, pp. 122–141;

Chiu Wai Boon (Zhao Weiben 赵维本), *YiJing Suyuan—Xiandai Wuda Zhongwen Shengjing Fanyishi* 译经溯源——现代五大中文圣经翻译史 (Tracing Bible Translation—A History of the Translation of Five Modern Chinese Versions of the Bible) (Hong Kong: China Graduate School of Theology, 1993), pp. 95–115. In this chapter, this Bible edition is referred to as the Today's Chinese Version.

34. Multiple answers and maximum three responses were allowed.

35. One response only was allowed.

36. Multiple answers were allowed.

37. Multiple answers and maximum three responses allowed.

38. In this section, the biblical quotations in English are taken, for reference only, from the New American Bible, available at http://www.vatican.va/archive/ENG0839/_INDEX.HTM (accessed January 27, 2021).

39. *Sigao Shengjing* (the Studium Biblicum Version) translates the term *logo9* (or "Word") as *shengyan*; other Catholic translations, such as the Sheshan New Testament translation and the Pastoral Bible, opt for the term *dao*.

40. For details on this issue, see Romano, "Translating and Transplanting the Word of God in Chinese," pp. 167–194.

PART III

Evangelization

CHAPTER 5

Catholic Fishermen in the Qingpu District of Shanghai

Rachel Zhu Xiaohong

Abstract Although the local chorography holds their Catholic faith initiated from the early period of the Qing dynasty, other documents indicate that the ancestors of Qingpu fishermen had already accepted the Catholic faith in the late Ming dynasty. The fishermen in this district share some similarities with other fisherfolk in southern Jiangsu (Sunan) around Lake Tai and Yangcheng Lake in many liturgical practices, such as the ceremonies of death and penitence, and manifest some particularities that set them apart from the Catholic faithful in urban areas. Catholic beliefs and behavior have been crucial elements of the self-identity of the fishing population during urbanization, as they settled on the land and became townsfolk.

Keywords Qingpu fishermen · Catholic identity · Liturgy · Inculturation

R. Z. Xiaohong (✉)
Fudan University, Shanghai, China
e-mail: xiaohongzhu@fudan.edu.cn

© The Author(s), under exclusive license to Springer Nature
Singapore Pte Ltd. 2022
C. Y. Chu (ed.), *The Catholic Church, The Bible, and Evangelization
in China*, Christianity in Modern China,
https://doi.org/10.1007/978-981-16-6182-2_5

89

Introduction

The Dan People 蜑民 in South China and the fishermen of the Nine Family Names 九姓渔民 in Jiangsu and Zhejiang have never been a popular topic among historians. However, research into these special communities that are in some sense left over from the "untouchable" caste in the ancient hierarchy can break through the limits of the traditional selection of historical material and approach to historical studies of mainland China. Such research encourages taking the perspectives of folk consciousness, identity construction, and daily life, which have diversified the approaches to social history research and refreshed and enhanced the overall understanding of the history of traditional societies.[1]

The detailed research undertaken for this chapter concerning this local social community was inspired by historical research into the "untouchable" fishermen of Qinqpu. Although not all fishermen have belonged to the caste of untouchables,[2] as "people on water" the Qingpu 青浦 fishermen shared a similar marginal social status to the untouchables. Due to the traditional social class ideology, expressed as "the four classes of scholars, farmers, workers, and merchants are the cornerstones of a country" (see the "Xiaokuang" 小匡 passage of the ancient text known as the *Guanzi* 管子), fishermen were always at the lowest level of traditional Chinese society. Fishermen had no home but their boats and fishing were their only livelihood. They were dependent on luck, had no stable residence, lacked education, and were looked down upon even by the poorest people living ashore; in fact, "Never marry your daughter to a fisherman" is a common Chinese proverb. With the socialist reforms in China, the domain of agriculture was enlarged to include fishing within the five walks of life: "farming, forestry, animal husbandry, side-line production, and fishery." The political status of fishermen thus became equal with other people, despite their economic status remaining low.

The majority of fishermen in China are Daoists. According to the research presented in 2011 by Professor Xingyong Han,[3] Shanghai fishermen mostly came from Jiangsu Province, whereas those around the Hangzhou Bay area mostly came from Zhejiang Province. The latter group are mainly adherents to Buddhism and folk religions or Daoism. They worship statues of gods and spirits related to water and fish, and they also pay homage to their ancestors. However, most of the fishermen in the area of Qingpu in the west of Shanghai are Catholics. These Catholic fishermen originated from the same place as the fishermen in the southern part of Jiangsu, around Lake Tai and the cities of Wuxi and Suzhou. The presence and experience of these Catholic fishermen are very worthy of investigation and interpretation.

Shanghai is a very important Catholic diocese in mainland China. The most common topics of the few studies of the Catholic diocese of Shanghai have been the influence of Jesuits, the diocesan bishops, the complicated relationship between China and the Vatican, the educational institutes run by the Church, the Tou-Se-We orphanage, and the Ming convert Paul Guangqi Xu. Little attention has been paid to the faith of communities of Catholic fishermen and very few studies have been conducted on the beliefs of fishermen in Jiangnan, the southern part of the Yangtze River.[4] In view of this, and based on local gazettes, missionary histories, and the limited scholarship on the fishermen in southern Jiangsu, this chapter examines and restores the history of Catholics in Qingpu and discusses the current situation and characteristics of this relatively closed and unique faith community while drawing on fieldwork and data obtained from the Shanghai Municipal Archives.

The High Percentage of Fishermen Among the Catholic Faithful in Qingpu

The Qingpu administrative district (青浦区) is located in the southwest of Shanghai municipality, downstream of the Lake Tai basin and upstream of Huangpu. Within the area, there are 1,817 rivers and 21 lakes, among which the Dianshan Lake is shared with Jiangsu Province, with 75.4% of the lake area in Qingpu. The population of fishermen in Qingpu is little more than 2,000 households, or nearly 10,000 people, accounting for less than 1% of the region's population in the 1960s and 1970s.[5] From 1967 to 1977, encouraged and supported by the government, many fishermen moved to live on the shore and settled in permanent residences, establishing more than 10 fishing villages (dedicated communities of fishermen) in various towns and villages in Qingpu. With the process of urbanization and the restriction of fishing for the protection of Dianshan Lake as a water source, most young fishermen have subsequently given up fishing as a vocation.

At present, approximately 57,000 people in the entire district of Qingpu claim to be religious, with most claiming adherence to Buddhism, Daoism, Catholicism, or Protestant Christianity. Going back to the Tang dynasty, the majority of the faithful in this area have been followers of

Buddhism and Daoism, which now number about 32,000. Protestant Christians came into this area in the late Qing dynasty; the majority of these believers are farmers, with the Protestant population now at around 15,000. There are about 10,000 Catholics in Qingpu,[6] over 80% of whom are fishermen. We can say that it is only among fishermen that there is a majority of Catholics. According to 1980 statistics, there were more than 3,600 fishermen over the age of 18 in Qingpu's largest fishing township, of whom more than 80% were Catholic.[7] The proportion may have been even higher in some other areas.

How can this phenomenon be explained? The literature tackles this question using social class analysis, deploying concepts such as "spiritual starvation" and "material poverty," with the theory of absolute and relative deprivation used to explain the formation and characteristics of this particular group. However, this approach does not go far enough to account for the differences in expressions of Christianity between this group and other rural Catholics. The high ratio of the Catholic population in the area is obviously related to the third wave of Christian missionaries who entered China in the Ming dynasty. The Qingpu county gazette (1990) clearly states that Catholicism in Qingpu "was introduced to the county in the second year of the Kangxi reign of the Qing dynasty [1663], having a history of more than 300 years," but supplies no further details. The missionary activities of the Jesuit Frarcuis Brancati (潘国光, 1607–1671) in Shanghai and Philippe Couplet (柏应理, 1623–1693) in Songjiang 松江 and Jiading 嘉定 were very successful at the time, and the founding of Catholicism in Qingpu could be tracked back to them if this timeline is correct, but this requires more examination. Jesuit missionaries, represented by Matteo Ricci (利玛窦, 1552–1610), successfully brought the gospel into China in the late Ming dynasty. The famous scholar Xu Guangqi (徐光启, 1562–1633), a native of Shanghai, converted and became one of the Three Pillars of Chinese Catholicism at the end of the Ming dynasty, eventually taking the high position of Grand Scholar of Wide Knowledge Court and the Secretary of the Ministry of Rites. In 1608, while he was in mourning in his hometown, he invited Father Lazzaro Cattaneo (郭居静, 1560–1640) to preach in Shanghai. Hence, Catholicism spread in Shanghai because of the Xu family. Xu's granddaughter Candida married into the Xu family in Songjiang, where believers then began to appear. In 1627, during the Wanli reign of the Ming dynasty, when the so-called Nanjing Persecution occurred, Xu and the missionary Emmanuel Diaz (李玛诺, 1559–1639) decided together "to adopt this way of life in case of a persecution": that is, to hide in a fishing boat.[8] According to the letter of the missionary João Froes (伏若望, 1591–1638), when another round of persecutions began, Xu Guangqi did indeed ask his son and the priests to board a boat to take refuge, instructing his son to take enough silver with him so that he could take care of anything unexpected.[9] The then densely populated waterways offered both ease of transportation and natural protection. During the Qianlong Prohibition of the Qing dynasty, not all missionaries were evacuated. The faith of the Catholic fishermen of Shanghai and Suzhou was firmly rooted and they did their best to protect the two Jesuit missionaries who would later be martyred, Father Antoine Giuseppe Henriquez (黄安多, 1707?–1748) and Father Tristano Francesco de Attimis (谈方济, 1701?–1748): "The area is a fishing village, with a network of rivers and harbors, and many Catholics are boat people. The two priests lurked in their boats during the day and landed at night from the back door of the families. The Holy Mass and other sacraments were performed at night and dispersed at dawn."[10] The missionaries followed this strategy, and it is speculated that this resulted in the first group of fishermen followers.

Fishermen who took the boat as their home had no fixed place of residence and floated around. Several generations often lived in one boat. Only after the son married would he get his own boat. Before they settled on land in the 1960s, most of the fishermen were uneducated; as the saying went, "Nine and a half fishermen out of ten are illiterate." Being engaged only in fishing or raising fish, and not in the distribution and selling of fishery products, their daily interactions were limited to their own group of fishermen; as they rarely married "shore people," they formed a relatively closed and marginalized community. As fishermen did not have the means to receive an education and did not leave self-descriptions, the statement of the Qingpu local gazette that the Catholic faith in Qingpu began in the early Qing dynasty probably refers to the time when the Catholic converts first appeared on shore. Qingpu was once administered as a part of Jiangsu Province and belonged to the apostolic vicariate of Jiangnan. In addition, because of the mobility of the fishermen's work and their frequent interactions with one another, the Qingpu fishermen and the Sunan fishermen in southern Jiangsu Province embraced the Catholic faith at around the same time, beginning from the late Ming dynasty.

According to the Jesuit missionary J. de la Servière (史式徽), "Since the seventeenth and eighteenth centuries, the fishermen of South Jiangsu have been organized into many prosperous communities."[11] In the second year of the Kangxi emperor's reign (1663), one such community, Changshu 常熟, had more than 10,000 Catholics, most of whom were fishermen.[12] From the founding of the Republic of China until just before 1949, more than half of the fishermen in southern Jiangsu were Catholics, and by the end of the 1940s, there were already 26,981 Catholics in the five counties of the diocese of Suzhou, among whom 14,000 were fishermen.[13] In some villages and towns, all of the fishermen were Catholics.[14] In Wuxi 无锡 in the 1940s, there were more than 20,000 Catholics, 86% of whom were fishermen (the remainder were farmers, merchants, and laborers). Among the fisherman of the so-called "inland waterways gang," two-thirds were Catholic.[15] Given these similarities, we can indeed study the fishermen of Wuxi, Suzhou, and Qingpu with the same frame of reference as that used by former researchers.

TRADITIONAL LIFE OF QINGPU CATHOLIC FISHERMEN

1. Daily life of the Catholic fishermen

The fishermen of Qingpu and Kunshan in southern Jiangsu are similar in their habits.[16] According to the recollections of the Kunshan clergy, the local net-boat fishermen can be divided into net-twisters (*nianwang bang* 捻网帮) and animal-catchers (*zhuosheng bang* 捉牲帮).[17] The same division can be made for the fishermen in Qingpu. The so-called net-twisters are those who use fishing nets to catch fish. Apart from the twisted wire fishnet, they use all kinds of other instruments to help catch blackfish, turtles, shrimps, and crabs. These fishermen have lived in the Yangcheng Lake, Lake Tai, and Dianshan Lake basins for generations. The animal-catchers mainly catch eels, turtles, mussels, silk snails, and even weasels in rivers or rice paddies. It is said that these people mainly came from northern Jiangsu. The earliest Catholic fishermen would have been the former kind; they were also known as net-boat Catholics (*wangchuan jiaoyou* 网船教友) in Shanghai. The animal-catchers might have slowly accepted Catholicism due to marriages into net-twister families. According to Father Jiang Huangji, former parish priest in Zhujiajiao, the few non-believers among the fishermen in that area were mostly animal-catchers. Net-boat fishermen generally have two boats: one large boat for household use and another small boat for business. The fishermen had large families, and it was not unusual for them to have five or six children. The children were baptized before they were 8 days old. When a boy was old enough to marry and received the sacrament of matrimony, a new boat was made to separate the new family from his parents.

Peasants were extremely poor in China in the first half of the twentieth century, but fishermen were destitute. Fishermen are said to have suffered from "seven bitternesses and fifteen taxations." The seven bitternesses refer to exploitation and bullying by the Japanese invaders, the government, soldiers, those in charge of dams and fish markets, and onshore gangsters; the fifteen taxations refer to exorbitant taxes and levies, namely "taxes for boat licenses and fish licenses, poll tax, bridging boards tax, outpost tax, military service tax, overhead expenses, guns and rice tax, pao-chia system tax, surface traffic expense, license, permits, certificates, waterway entry tax, annual festivals, and water crossings tax."[18] Exploited in so many ways, the fishermen were politically helpless and economically destitute. Their working environment was very harsh, with no shelter from the wind and rain while working and traveling in water. There was a saying in the Dianshan Lake area: "Nine out of ten nets are empty; only one net has some fish jumping in." Moreover, the area around Qingpu was seriously affected by schistosomiasis. Even in the 1960s, boarding schools set up especially for the children of fishermen could not attract students, because the fishermen could not afford the expense for schooling and could not spare even one quilt for their child, with many fishermen only having one quilt to share among the whole family.[19]

During the socialist transformation beginning in 1949, the democratic reform movement was relevant to fishermen. Those on large ships that had a trade union organized themselves into fishing vessel unions, those who had large boats for transporting fertilizer and for business organized into boatmen's associations, and small seagoing vessels organized into fishermen's associations[20]; there were no such organizations, however, for Catholic fisherman. In 1953, the county of Qingpu piloted fishermen's mutual aid groups to help them out of poverty. In 1956, a fisheries co-operative was established finally in Qingpu, in which the nets were collectively owned and distributed according to individual work, and fishermen were paid at a fixed rate. There was even a pilot project to distribute a production quota to households and give them an extra payment share in times of overproduction. At the end of 1958, Qingpu established a fishery people's commune, the Liberation Commune, as a production base and 16 aquatic products brigades under the jurisdiction of the rural people's commune as distribution hubs. In the 1960s, surface aquaculture began. What really improved fishermen's lives, however, was the construction of fishing villages, which began in 1966 and was further promoted in 1973. Through interest-free loans and self-financing, and with construction materials provided by the government as a priority, the fishing villages were expanded and renovated through to the mid-1980s.[21] Since the various forms of co-contracting developed in the 1980s, fishermen have also shifted from simple fishing to a breeding-based production model, which has resulted in much higher incomes and a real improvement in their lives. In one interview, a fisherman in his eighties said, "Without the Communist Party and the government, it is unbelievable that we could live in a house on the shore from living in a boat."

2. Religious life of the Catholic fishermen

Historically, Qingpu Catholic fishermen mainly gathered in the three parishes of Tailaiqiao 泰莱桥, Yangziyu 杨字圩, and Zhujiajia 朱家角, all of which had subordinate gathering places. The parish of Yangziyu was founded first, with around 1,500 fishermen and 200 peasants. When Father Frarcuis Brancati was preaching in the Jiangnan area he laid down a tradition of grouping parishioners into different confraternities according to their ages and vocations.[22] The fishermen parishioners in Jiangnan were grouped into confraternities based on their region. Each small group elected a leader who was responsible for communication and assisted the priests in dealing with religious affairs among the group. Each year when the Church hosted catechism classes, the group leader would encourage parents to send their children to the local church to study the catechism, thus ensuring that children received a basic religious education; they also arranged pilgrimages and monitored attendance to the main feasts.[23] For the four major Church festivals, Christmas, Easter, the Pentecost, and the Assumption of Mary, the "boats filled all the rivers around the church."[24]

The traditional Catholic fishermen were very enthusiastic and especially fond of icons.[25] In the main cabin of the fishing boat, there was a corner altar decorated with a crucifix and icons of the Sacred Heart of Jesus, the

Virgin Mary, angels, and saints, some of which were placed in a wooden box in the shape of a tabernacle with a glass cover and candles or plastic flowers on both sides. The Catholic fishermen observed the divine hour strictly. The lauds and vespers were times for the whole family to gather in front of the altar: "It was so refreshing to hear them recite the rosary in a loud voice as their ships passed by or moored among the other ships of non-believers," recorded J. de la Servière.[26] Most fishermen were illiterate, but they could recite entire texts of the Divine Office or the Rosary by heart.[27] One passage in the popular local hymn, "Song of Our Lady of Qingyang," reflects the fervor to venerate the Virgin Mary among the Catholic fishermen working in the lower courses of the Yangtze River: "Changzhou, Jiangyin, Wuxi, Yixing, everywhere, worship the Mother of God. You come to reverence, I come to praise, praise and reverence to our Mother in Heaven. Catholics on boats, Catholics on shore, with all hearts and souls, come to pray."

The Catholic fishermen also made an annual pilgrimage to Sheshan, where fishermen from Qingpu, Wuxi, and Suzhou were predominant among the pilgrims. "In every May, the holy month dedicated to Our Lady of Mary, the fishermen moor their boats on the river at the foot of Sheshan Mountain for several days. Every early morning, families go up the hill on pilgrimage. After stopping in the chapel at the halfway of the hill, they would follow the Via Dolorosa and pay homage before the stations of the cross, and join the mass in the basilica on the top of the Sheshan, while they take the sacrament of reconciliation, and receive Holy Communion. After the Mass, they go back to chapel and spent hours to prayers in front of three pavilions dedicated to the holy family."[28] The pilgrimage took longer and involved more elaborate activities than other religious events. According to the memoir of the deceased Bishop Aloysius Jin Luxian of the diocese of Shanghai,[29] when he was young he went on a pilgrimage to Sheshan by boat. He saw many boats, especially fishing boats, and many Catholic fishermen and their children near the entrance at the foot of the Sheshan Mountain. At night, he could hear the vespers from the fishing boats. The fishing families were plainly dressed, many even wearing patched clothes, but they were generous in terms of donations and Mass offerings.

A Catholic clergyman once explained the reason that the fishermen were Catholics: "Because they live a simple life, having simple thoughts and are generous to others, it is easy for them to resonate with the teachings of love God and to love people in the Catholic faith. At the same time, the fishermen are of a rough and straightforward nature, sincere, trustworthy and unpretentious, and once they accept the Catholic faith, they are faithful to the end and remain faithful until death."[30] This statement is supported by their high degree of loyalty to the priests and to the teachings of the Church.[31] Living on fishing boats and marginalized from the social life of the shore dwellers, the fishermen lived an isolated cultural life. Once the set pattern of a life of Catholic faith was accepted, there was little chance of it being changed by influences from the outside world, which explains to some extent their religious fidelity. In addition, the isolated fishermen, who were used to struggling alone, lacked the bonds formed by social and collective activities, and the Catholic liturgy brought them together, giving them a complete identity and spiritual comfort.

PRESENT LIFE OF CATHOLIC FISHERMEN

1. A new living space for fishermen: The fishing villages

Beginning in the early 1960s, prompted and facilitated by the government, these fishermen began to settle ashore. There is now a similar fishing village in each of the 11 towns and sub-districts of Qingpu. The three churches of Tailaiqiao, Yangziyu, and Zhujiajiao still exist; the Yangziyu church is now under the supervision of the Zhujiajiao parish (it was formerly under the Tailaiqiao parish) and the Tailaiqiao church is the deanery office for Qingpu. According to ecclesiastic tradition, some of the Catholic fishermen of Diandong, a town in the Kunshan county of Jiangsu Province, still belong to the Zhujiajiao parish.

The Catholic fishermen used to reside on their boats, which drifted in the water and gave them no fixed address, but they all belonged to parishes and strictly observed the four precepts of the Church. Marriages, deaths, baptisms, and confirmations related to the families of the Catholic fishermen were strictly recorded and reported to the diocese, as was church attendance, mainly at festivals. Now that fishermen parishioners have settled ashore, their former transportation to church by boat is no longer easily accessible due to urban development. To make it easier for senior Catholics who have difficulty traveling, the Qingpu deanery office has set up several "prayer houses" in Jinze 金泽, Chonggu重固, Fengxi 凤溪, Baihe白鹤, Xianghuaqiao香花桥, Huaxin华新, and Zhaotun赵屯, where priests regularly deliver Mass.

Fishing villages were built in Chonggu and Huaxin in the early 1970s for fishermen to settle ashore. These do not have the largest populations of the existing fishing villages, and the same priest, Father Liu Qiang, who is the rector of the diocesan Tailaiqiao Preparatory Seminary, is responsible for both. He presides over Mass on the second Sunday of each month in Huaxin, on the fourth Sunday of each month in Chonggu, and on special feast days. There used to be two larger fishing villages nearby: Baihe and Xianhuaqiao. Xianhuaqiao village has disappeared because of urban renewal, but Baihe is still active, with over 500 believers in about 200 families, and is managed by another priest from the Tailaiqiao deanery.

2. Religious spaces in the two fishing villages of Huaxin and Chonggu

There are over 80 households and 200 parishioners in the Huaxin fishing village and over 100 households and 300 parishioners in the Chonggu fishing village. Although each family still keeps fishing boats, only slightly more than 10 families are engaged in fishing. There are a few more households in Chonggu that continue to fish, most of whom are senior couples over 60 years old. Ten years ago, Huaxin began to use the assembly hall of the neighborhood committee as a place for prayer and to host Masses. Four years ago, Chonggu also began to have a prayer place in a family home.

The so-called prayer house in the Huaxin fishing village is in fact a public hall of the neighborhood committee (*juweihui* 居委会), a place where villagers invite guests for banquets during weddings and funerals. In rural Jiangnan before 1949, the ancestral hall was often the village meeting place. Later, the auditorium or public hall replaced the ancestral hall as a meeting place for commune members. With the decline of the commune system, general assemblies have become rare except for weddings and funerals. Feasts for a small number of people could be held in the open space in front of and behind family houses, but the auditorium is perfect for a large dinner party. A few years ago, peasant villagers were reluctant to use the site because they feared their good luck might be washed away as the fishermen often used this place for religious ceremonies. With the increasing cost of renting other places, they have come to accept the reality of sharing the auditorium with the Catholics.[32]

The prayer house in Huaxin is truly a place where decay is transformed into magic. Normally, it is just a simple bungalow, until eager parishioners start to set up the auditorium before the liturgy begins. There is a holy water basin on the left of the entrance and a confession booth on the right. Church drapes are hung on the walls of both sides. Black drapes are hung for memorials and different colored drapes for different Masses. A wooden door and niche in the back wall of the south altar become backdrops for the main altar, which is creatively set up as a long table covered with white folded cloth, and movable benches and round stools are arranged in rows as pews for the faithful; none of the elements that a church needs are missing. Before Mass begins and after it ends, the fishermen split up to handle the various furnishings and vessels stored in the sacristy, which is a small storage room at the back left of the hall. They quickly lay out their own sanctuary, changing an ordinary place into a sacred space.

In the Chonggu fishing village, according to the local priest, Father Liuqiang, most of the believers are not enthusiastic. Therefore, although the public hall in the village has been renovated, it remains empty and no religious activities are permitted inside. The few enthusiastic families take turns using their own living rooms and courtyards for Mass. Most of the houses in the fishing villages have the same structure: there is a small open or walled courtyard, a kitchen in the courtyard, a guest hall or parlor where fishing gear and sundries are stacked and guests are received, a bedroom for the elders on the first floor, and a bedroom for the young generation on the second floor. Often the kitchen becomes the priest's confession booth, the courtyard and parlor filled with benches become the chapel, the dining table in the parlor facing the entrance becomes the altar, and a crucifix and the icons of the Sacred Heart of Jesus or the Virgin Mary, which are the most common icons in the homes of the faithful, hung on the wall opposite the front door, serve as backdrops for the altar. A living space thus becomes a place of communion with God.

ELEMENTS OF INCULTURATION

The religious beliefs of the fishermen at the border of Jiangsu, Zhejiang, and Shanghai are not limited to Catholicism. Before the introduction of Catholicism, a folk religion combining elements of Confucianism, Taoism, and Buddhism was dominant among the fishermen. The Taoist goddess of heaven (*tianfei* 天妃), the deity of the city (*chenghuang* 城隍),

and the traditional King Yu (*Yu Wang* 禹王) all had their own worshippers. Some fishermen also believed in the I-Guan-Dao (*yiguandao* 一贯道) and the Hungmen Triad (*hongmen sanjiao* 洪门三教), which are defined by the government as evil cults.[33] Polytheistic faiths, such as Buddhism and Taoism, are still dominant in the rural areas of Qingpu. On major festivals, village temples abound with incense and offerings of all kinds of food, such as pig head, chicken, fish, and fruit, are piled up before statues of gods and Buddha. Relatively, Qingpu fishermen keep the Catholic faith in a more particular way.

Compared to urban Catholics, Catholic fishermen place more emphasis on the Mass offering and the sacrament of reconciliation. Before each Mass, people queue for a very long time to contribute to the Mass offering and then to take the sacrament of penance. On special holidays (mainly Christmas and Easter), they, like the temple congregation, offer goods, such as fish, shrimp, and milk, to the Church. Whereas the disciples of folk religions make offerings to their gods and spirits, Catholic believers offer the food to the monastic priests to thank them for their efforts and support evangelization in the local community.

As few fishermen had access to school before moving onto the shore, almost all of the fishermen over 60 years old are illiterate. There is one senior fisherman over 80 years old who can read; his parents sent him to stay in the parish school on the invitation of the priest. Most of the Catholic fishermen of the older generation are able to say common prayers, such as the Rosary, and appropriate prayers for special occasions. Church doctrines and the Catholic faith have been passed down from generation to generation among these illiterate fishermen through these prayers. Normally, the fishermen gather at least one and half hours before each Mass to say the prayers together and prepare their hearts to join the holy communion. The congregation responds loudly with the prayer when the priest lifts the cup and bread during the liturgy of Eucharist. After the Mass, the fishermen pray loudly to express the thanksgiving and the intercession for the dead.

After each Mass, the priest changes the chasuble and begins the memorial liturgy right away. A standard liturgical book is used for this liturgy of the dead, containing special prayers and local hymns. This liturgy for the remembrance of the dead has been very common in the churches in the mission of Jiangnan, and many churches in the dioceses of Shanghai, Suzhou, and Nanjing maintain this tradition today, with slight differences in application. Most churches in Shanghai have a chapel dedicated to memorials after Mass. Regardless of how long ago a loved one passed away, believers can bring their own supplicate intentions and pray with the priest in a memorial to remember the deceased. For example, on All Souls' Day in 2014, the first liturgy of memorial ceremony hosted by Father Liu was dedicated to two bishops of Shanghai, Bishop Aloysius Jin Luxian, who passed away in 2013, and Bishop Joseph Fan Zhongliang, who passed away in 2014. The importance of the unity of the Church during extraordinary times for the diocese was thus emphasized to the Catholic fishermen. The second memorial was dedicated to loved ones who had died less than 1 year before or who were close to the anniversary of their death. The third liturgy was for all of the other deceased in the community.

Chinese traditional religions maintain a belief that people go to the underworld after they die. For their well-being in this other world, and for them to bless their living families with fortune and prosperity, people are very cautious about death and take funeral rituals very seriously, believing in serving the dead as if they were alive. The fishermen follow the tradition of holding a special memorial ceremony on the seventh day after their family members die, on each seventh day thereafter, on the hundredth day, on the first anniversary, and so on. Like others around them, they wear white mourning clothing; female family members wear a head decoration of red thread and white flowers and male family members a hemp rope around their waists. For the Catholics, however, there are no farmers and villagers burning joss paper and no Taoists or monks holding ceremonies. Instead, priests are invited to be present, giving a memorial Mass together with fellow village believers and relatives in church. The children and relatives of the deceased who invite the priests also hire a cook to prepare a grand meal to be enjoyed by all attendees after the Mass.

LAST WORDS: FAITH LEGACY AND IDENTITY

The Catholic fishermen of Qingpu, once the lowest group in the social hierarchy, moved onto the land in the 1970s to settle in the fishing villages designated for them by the government, before moving into renovated and self-built buildings in the 20 years thereafter. Another 20 years later, because of the compensation given by the government for taking away their private land for urban development, they can now afford to live in third-generation apartments in skyscrapers with elevators, no different from city people. Under the harsh conditions of religion being forbidden, the fishermen did not give up their faith, but now they live comfortably in the reformed and open social environment, new challenges have arisen: rebellious youth would rather stay home watching television or surfing the Internet than go to church; the middle-aged are working in other places, or working overtime on the weekends, and reluctant to go to church; and seniors sometimes skip the monthly Mass if prices are high in the fish market. To accommodate these new situations, the deanery and the priests not only hold Masses in the villages, but they also organize frequent pilgrimages to various places, providing their parishioners with more time and opportunity to experience the communal life of faith, and arrange various activities and Bible lessons for children in the fishing villages during the summer break, encouraging children to learn from a young age the faith of their grandparents.

In reality, the Qingpu fishing community is continuously contracting. Fishing is restricted or forbidden by policies to protect the Dianshan Lake as a water source and some waterways and rivers are polluted. With the fishing area thus reduced, middle-aged fishermen have left the vocation of their ancestors; with a limited education, most have become factory workers or community service providers. Their ancestors left them the legacy of faith, and they exhibit an even-tempered and kindhearted character, but the young generation does not have the passion or opportunity to engage in fishing. The Catholic faith brought to the Qingpu fishermen a different identity and experience, and as the fishermen identity disappears, the Catholic faith will become the only distinct feature of this particular group of people living in this area with a special history. In the course of social transition, how specific elements, especially the element of religion, will be involved in the construction of identity and how they will affect the social life of the group are the direction for future research in this project.

Acknowledgement My heartfelt gratitude goes to Father Jiang Huangji of the Shanghai Catholic diocese, from whom I received timely and precious advice in the course of writing this chapter, and to Father Liu Qiang and Mi Liang, who generously helped me and warmly guided me in my research. My friend Ms. Liyue Zhang helped with the draft Chinese translation. Research for this paper was supported by the Ministry of Education Humanities and Social Sciences Research Planning Project 19YJA730008 and Shanghai Social Sciences Planning Project 2018BZX001.

NOTES

1. Zhang Xiaoye, "Establishment and Idea: The Remodeling the Fishermen of Nine Family Names from the Outcast to the Good People," *Journal of Social Science*, No. 4 (2006), p. 174.
2. The untouchable caste appeared in the Tang dynasty and was strengthened in the Ming dynasty. Although there was reform during the Qing dynasty to raise the status of this group up to that of common people, the new status took a long time to be acknowledged as social attitudes were slow to change. The concept of "untouchable" was not yet uprooted even in the Republic of China.
3. See Han Xingyong, "Religious Faith and Living Culture of Fishermen—A Comparative Study on the Religious Beliefs of Fishermen in Zhejiang, Jiangsu and Shanghai," *Proceedings of 2011 Annual Convention of Chinese Sociology and the Second Marine Sociology Forum*, pp. 257–264.
4. Only six articles related to the religious aspects of fishermen in Jiangsu and Zhejiang have appeared: Gaoliang, "Customs and Religious Beliefs of Fishermen in Old Jiangsu," *Ancient and Modern Agriculture*, No. 2 (1991), pp. 70–79; Shi Guoming and Song Bingliang, "A Preliminary Inquiry into the Catholic Faith of Fishermen in Southern Jiangsu," *Journal of Religious Studies*, No. 9 (1987), pp. 79–84; Li Yong and Chi Zihua, "The Catholic Faith of Fishermen in Modern Southern Jiangsu," *Chinese Agricultural History*, No. 4 (2006), pp. 98–104; Han Xingyong, "Religious Faith and Living Culture"; Rachel Zhu Xiaohong, "Catholic Faith in Qing-pu Fishermen's Identity-Building," *Christian Thought Review*, series 21 (Beijing: Religious Culture Press, 2016), pp. 467–481; Liqiang, "Suffering and Waiting for Change: The Daily Life of Catholic Fishermen and Faithful Around Shanghai During the Second World War," *Pengpai News*, July 14, 2020, http://m.thepaper.cn/rss_newsDetail_7952940?from=.
5. It says that "there are about 2,000 households, or 9300 people in 17 communes" in a report Qingpu County Geming Commission to Shanghai Municipal Geming Commission in 1968, see Shanghai Municipal Archives, "The Schedule of Implementing Land Settlement for Fishermen in the Family Fishing Boat" (1968), Archive QingGe (68), document no. 83; here is another record that there

were about 2045 households in Qingpu district in a report from Municipal Aquatic Bureau to Municipal Finance and Economic Section in 1976, "Report on the Funds and Materials Needed for the Land Settlement of Fishermen on Family Fishing Boats in Suburban Areas" (1976), Archive HuShuiGe (76), document no. 186.

6. According to the Shanghai Qingpu District United Front Work Department of the Communist Party of China, in 2006 the population of Catholics was 10,000; see "Religions in Qingpu District," http://tz.shqp.gov.cn/gb/content/2006-07/20/content_108448.htm, accessed November 3, 2016. At present, the official website does not provide more accurate or up-to-date figures.

7. Han Xingyong, "Religious Faith and Living Culture," p. 260.

8. Augustinus Colombels, *Histoire de la mission du Kiang-nan*, vol. 2, trans. Zhou Shiliang (Taipei: Fuda shufang, 2013), p. 548.

9. João Froes, "Paul Xu Jinshi Memoirs" (1634), trans. Dong Shaoxin, *Journal of Studies of Macau History*, No. 6 (2007), p. 157.

10. Fanghao, *Biographies of Chinese Catholic People* (Shanghai: Catholic Diocese of Shanghai Guangqi Press, 2003), p. 567.

11. J. de la Servière, *Histoire de la mission du Kiang-nan* [Chinese version], vol. 2, trans. Historical Material Group of Shanghai Catholic Diocese (Shanghai: Shanghai Yiwen Press, 1983), p. 244.

12. J. de la Servière, *Histoire de la mission du Kiang-nan* [Chinese version], vol. 1, p. 22.

13. Shi Guoming and Song Bingliang, "An Exploration of the Catholic Faith of Fishermen in Southern Jiangsu," *Religious Studies*, No. 9 (1987), pp. 79–84.

14. Editorial Committee for the Local Gazette of Wu County, Suzhou, *The Local Gazette of Wu County* (Shanghai: Shanghai Guji Publishing House, 1994). For this article, refer to the official website of the Suzhou local gazette, http://www.dfzb.suzhou.gov.cn/zsbl/451427.htm, accessed on November 3, 2015.

15. Liyong and Chi Zhihua, "The Catholic Faith of Modern Sunan Fishermen," *Agricultural History of China*, No. 4 (2006), p. 100.

16. Jesuit Francois Tsu's doctoral thesis at the University of Paris in 1948, which explored fishermen on the lower Yangtze River, pointed out that the boats of fishermen in different areas had

different shapes. Therefore, experienced fishermen could determine the origin of other fishermen at a glance. However, the boats of Qingpu and Kunshan were of the same shape. Francois Xavier Tsu (朱树德) S. J., "A vie des pêcheur du Bas Yang-Tse[M]," Ph.D. dissertation, University of Paris, 1948.

17. Ji Fuxiang, *Hand in Hand with God until the Ends of the Earth: The Memoirs of Father Ji Fuxiang* (unpublished, 2005), p. 7.
18. Liyong and Chi Zhihua, "The Catholic Faith of Modern Sunan Fishermen," p. 102.
19. Shanghai Municipal Archives, "Report on the Enrolment of the Children of Fishermen in Qingpu, Jiading and Songjiang Counties," 1965.
20. Shanghai Municipal Archives, "Report: Shanghai Committee Boat Office 53'1055," 1953.
21. Editorial Committee of Qingpu Local Gazetteers, "Chapter 33, Religious, Nationalities, Overseas Chinese Affairs, Foreign Affairs," *Qingpu County Local Gazette* (Shanghai: Shanghai People's Publishing House, 1990), for this article refer to the official website of the Shanghai Local Gazetteers Office, http://www.shtong.gov.cn/node2/node4/node2250/node4427/node5607/node11605/node11620/userobject1ai19109.html (accessed November 3, 2020).
22. C.f. Fanghao, *Biographies of Chinese Catholic People*, p. 280; J. de la Servière, *Histoire de la mission du Kiang-nan* [Chinese Version], vol. 1, pp. 252–53. Daniel Bays, the famous American historian of the Chinese Church, makes the observation that the solid foundation laid by the Jesuit and other religious missionaries of the seventeenth century, and lasted until the first half of the nineteenth century, explains the Chinese Catholics remained faithful to the Church for several generations, no matter the local or national persecution or the sharp decline of the European missionaries. Daniel Bays, *A New History of Chinese Christianity* (Oxford: Wiley-Blackwell, 2012), p. 35.
23. Ji Fuxiang, *Hand in Hand with God*, p. 8.
24. J. de la Servière, *Histoire de la mission du Kiang-nan* [Chinese Version], vol. 1, p. 253.
25. J. de la Servière, *Histoire de la mission du Kiang-nan* [Chinese Version], vol. 2, p. 245.

26. J. de la Servière, *Histoire de la mission du Kiang-nan* [Chinese Version], vol. 1, p. 254.
27. As described by the scholars who were able to visit the fishing boats in the early 1990s, "When reciting the rosary, they hold a string of beads in their hands and pluck one bead for each Ave Maria until the rosary is finished." See Ruan Renze and Gao Zhennong, eds., *History of Shanghai Religions* (Shanghai: Shanghai People's Publishing House, 1992), p. 664.
28. Ruan Renze and Gao Zhennong, eds., *History of Shanghai Religions*, p. 664.
29. Jin Luxian, *Jin Luxian wenji* (Shanghai: Shanghai Dictionary Press, 2007), p. 243.
30. Ji Fuxiang, *Hand in Hand with God*, p. 6.
31. Shanghai Municipal Archives, "Report on the Enrolment of the Children of Fishermen in Qingpu, Jiading and Songjiang Counties," Shanghai Municipal Archives (1965), p. 3.
32. However, very few farmers around the Catholic fishing villages convert to Catholicism, and intermarriage between the two communities is relatively rare. The fishermen families generally used to seek marriage partners within Catholicism, and couples in their forties or older are mostly intermarried with Catholic fishermen in the Sunan–Shanghai region. The younger generation now might marry the girls from other cities or regions, and only in this case will there be new converts.
33. Han Xingyong, "Religious Faith and Living Culture," p. 259.

CHAPTER 6

Between Survival and Subordination: Jiangnan Catholics in the 1950s

Steven Pieragastini

Abstract This chapter explores the complex relationship between Jiangnan Catholics and the Chinese Communist Party (CCP) in the 1950s. The new regime was eager to court the Catholic community to promote the Catholic Reform Movement, which formed the basis for the Chinese Catholic Patriotic Association (CCPA). However, Catholics proved reluctant to break ranks to denounce missionaries, provoke a schism with Rome, or sacrifice basic elements of their faith. In the late 1950s, Jiangnan Catholics were targeted heavily during the Anti-Rightist Campaign and the CCPA was established with much fanfare and the overt support of many Catholics. However, archival documents reveal that many "patriotic" Catholics sought means of advocating their faith within the constraints set by the CCP.

S. Pieragastini (✉)
Independent Scholar, Los Angeles, CA, USA

© The Author(s), under exclusive license to Springer Nature
Singapore Pte Ltd. 2022
C. Y. Chu (ed.), *The Catholic Church, The Bible, and Evangelization in China*, Christianity in Modern China,
https://doi.org/10.1007/978-981-16-6182-2_6

109

Keywords Church-state relations · Shanghai · Catholic Church · Chinese Communist Party (CCP) · Chinese Catholic Patriotic Association (CCPA)

INTRODUCTION

As is well known to scholars of Christianity in China, the Jiangnan region has been an important center of Chinese Catholicism for centuries. Early converts to the Church included esteemed officials of the Ming dynasty, most notably Xu Guangqi, who was a native of Shanghai. The families and extended social networks of these Ming literati formed the basis of the Church in the region and sustained it throughout periodic suppression of Christianity in the mid-Qing era. In particular, the counties surrounding Shanghai (now districts of the Shanghai municipality), such as Qingpu and Songjiang, were the bedrock of the wider Catholic community in Jiangnan. Following the First Opium War (1839–1842), Christianity became officially tolerated and Shanghai became the financial, organizational, and cultural center of Catholicism in China. A number of scholars have examined the history of the Church in Jiangnan during the late Ming and early Qing periods, and a few works have touched on these important Catholic communities in the late nineteenth and early twentieth centuries. However, much less has been written about the recent history of Jiangnan Catholics, especially since the founding of the People's Republic in 1949.

Drawing on archival research, this paper explores the complex relationship between Jiangnan Catholics (both clergy and laity) and the Chinese Communist Party (CCP) in the early years of the Maoist era. The new regime was eager to court the Catholic community to promote the Catholic Reform Movement, which formed the basis for the Chinese Catholic Patriotic Association (CCPA). However, Catholics proved reluctant to break ranks to denounce missionaries, provoke a schism with Rome, or sacrifice basic elements of their faith. This uneasy relationship went through periods of greater and lesser tension in the early to mid-1950s, guided by wider geopolitical phenomena, such as the Korean War and the reaction of the Holy See to global communism. In the late 1950s, Jiangnan Catholics were targeted heavily during the Anti-Rightist Campaign and the CCPA was established with much fanfare and the ostensible support of many Catholics. However, archival documents reveal that this acquiescence was superficial, and even many "patriotic" Catholics sought means of advocating their faith within the constraints set by the CCP.

THE EARLY YEARS OF THE PEOPLE'S REPUBLIC OF CHINA

Following the Second Sino-Japanese War (1937–1945), the Catholic Church in Jiangnan and throughout China seemed destined for a new, hopeful era of development, or even a "Catholic Renaissance." The war had destroyed churches, hospitals, and schools, severely weakened the Church's robust financial base, and placed the Church in a difficult political position; but it also provided a clean slate by erasing the overt connections between the Church and imperialism, settling the Rites Controversy, and laying the groundwork for an indigenous, national hierarchy. The Sino-Japanese conflict was an arduous political trial for the Church in China, but by the war's end, its relationship with the Nationalist government was more secure than ever. However, the Communists posed an ominous and increasing threat, with widespread attacks on Catholics in northern China in 1946 and 1947. Fortunately, the CCP's pursuit of United Front policies late in the Civil War period provided room for mutual toleration between Church and state in the first year of the People's Republic.

China's entry into the Korean War (1950–1953) greatly heightened Church–state tensions, leading to arrests of foreign missionaries, Chinese priests, and lay Catholics, as well as the appropriation of the Church's educational and charitable institutions and the weakening of its financial base in real estate. Concurrently, the Vatican launched a full-throated denunciation of communism and forbade clergy in China from cooperating with the new People's Government, effectively turning them into "Fifth Columnists." Tensions peaked during a 1951 campaign against the Legion of Mary 圣母军, a lay youth organization that the CCP viewed as a front for counter-revolutionary activity. This campaign[1] coincided with a push for "patriotic" Catholics to establish a reform movement within the Church that ultimately served as the basis for the CCPA. It was also simultaneous to the Land Reform Movement, which directly threatened the finances of the Church.

The tensions of the Korean War era can be seen through a close examination of one of the many Catholic communities in the villages surrounding Shanghai. By the Party's own admission, the Church was an "instrumental" part of people's lives in these communities well into the 1950s. The case of Qibao七宝镇 in Longhua district (now Minhang) demonstrates how difficult it could be to enact the Party's mass politics, veneration of struggle, and interminable campaigns in the face of unified opposition. At the time of the Liberation, there were over 2,000 Catholics in Longhua district, most of whom were poor peasants. These communities lived together in several clusters, the most prominent of which was the hamlet of Gujiatang 顾家堂村in Dianxun 电讯乡, which was within the Catholic parish of Qibao but maintained five small chapels (*tangkou* 堂口) of its own. According to a 1955 report on the area by the Party Committee for Shanghai's Suburbs 中共上海市郊区工作委员会, the Catholic peasants of the area had long been under the "complete control" of priests in Xujiahui and, because of "religious superstition," some 13 pious women and men went unmarried, devoting themselves to religious activities. The entire community suffered from "low consciousness" and "backwards thinking."[2]

Before the CCP took over administration of the area, the "reactionary priest" in Qibao, Fu Hezhou 傅鹤洲, warned his parishioners during Mass that the Communists were destroying churches and restricting religious activity in northern China. In response, Fu's flock began to hide their idols and paint crosses with the words "Lord Protect Us" (天主保佑) on the walls of their homes. Fu was also accused of scaring parishioners[3] with talk of U.S. atomic weapons and the possibility of the conflict in Korea setting off a Third World War, which was a surefire way to get oneself labeled a reactionary at the time. After Fu relocated to Shanghai to manage the finances of the diocese,[4] the parish priest was one Father John Zhang Weihan 张维翰, who was also considered by the Party to be a "reactionary priest" who practiced "false charity" by helping peasants till their fields or finding money for poor families (which was interpreted as a deliberate attempt to undermine the government's own program of loans to support production). Zhang's charity did, however, make him popular with his congregation, which is perhaps why he became the focal point of a spontaneous act of popular resistance by Qibao Catholics, the result of long-building tensions precipitated by an absurd misunderstanding.

In late January 1952, the town government's propaganda team planned to stage a Shanghainese opera, "The Man Who Sold His Soul" (出卖灵魂的人), at the main church in Qibao, but wisely decided to consult with Zhang first. Zhang told them he would need to ask his congregation, and when he did so during Mass the following Sunday, the congregation resolutely refused. Immediately following Mass, the propaganda team invited Zhang to the town government building to negotiate a solution, but rumors began to spread that Zhang had been arrested. Within hours, roughly a thousand Catholics from throughout the area had descended on the town center in Qibao and surrounded the town government building, holding an impromptu vigil that quickly turned into a demonstration against the government. The villagers, egged on by "registered landlords, wealthy peasants, and counter-revolutionaries," chanted slogans about religious freedom and the abuse of Catholics, defiantly shouting "the government has masses, we have masses too; let's see whose power is greater!"[5] Tensions were gradually calmed after the government produced Father Zhang and held negotiations with him and a group of demonstration leaders. In the following weeks, the "landlords" behind the demonstration were arrested by the government.[6]

This incident was associated with the rollout of the Land Reform Movement in Qibao, which was a minor disaster. After registering parcels of land and instituting two rounds of rent reductions beginning in late 1949, land reform began in Qibao in the winter of 1951–1952 (some months later than in the surrounding non-Catholic villages). Although the struggle began as planned and landlords were stripped of their lands, the masses did not rise up as expected. The peasants in the town likewise "lacked enthusiasm" when prompted to participate in campaigns to increase agricultural production[7] and in corvée labor drives to protect against insects and natural disasters. Eventually, Church properties in Qibao were appropriated (征收) and "made communal" (共有房产) via distribution to Catholic villagers, although some were reluctant to accept any redistributed land, perhaps because of the Church's opposition to land reform as a form of theft forbidden by the Ten Commandments. In the course of land reform, Ignatius Gong Pinmei, the Bishop of Shanghai, had protected two Catholic "despotic landlords" (恶霸地主), including one of the ringleaders of the January 1952 demonstration. It was later alleged that Gong made photographic copies of the landlords' deeds (田契) to nearly 200 mu of land[8] and sent them abroad for safekeeping, along with photos of Church property deeds, on the presumption that the Guomindang would one day return and allow property holders to reclaim their land. After their landholdings were redistributed to peasants, Gong had Fu Hezhou give the "landlords" 200 yuan out of "compassion."[9]

In the following years, the local government and party cadres had continual problems with the Catholics of Qibao. By 1955, some

35 counter-revolutionaries had been arrested or subjected to struggle sessions, including 18 in Gujiatang alone (a hamlet consisting of 93 Catholic households). Catholics, including a junior army officer, were accused of disrupting the process of establishing agricultural cooperatives, which, it was hoped, would increase production and thereby smooth over religiopolitical tensions. These tensions were played out weekly in Mass through the politics of the Eucharist, witnessed elsewhere in the course of the 1950s (and since), in which "reactionary" priests would deny Communion (停领圣体) to "patriotic" Catholics or "patriotic" priests would deny Communion to "reactionary" Catholics.[10]

BALANCING ACT

Even amid these harsh confrontations, which were common throughout Jiangnan and elsewhere in China, there were efforts by the government to placate Catholics and support Catholic institutions in the hope of encouraging an anti-Vatican reform movement in the Church. The CCP's ultimate repression of the Shanghai Catholic Church seems predictable when examined superficially, but an in-depth investigation shows that the Party's policy vacillated between reluctant tolerance, repression, and co-optation.

The failure of the 1951 campaign against the Legion of Mary left a shroud of uncertainty over the Church in Shanghai. Clergy and laity alike were incensed by the campaign and especially by the death of Zhang Boda and a number of other priests, along with the imprisonment of dozens more. A more relaxed political environment following the end of the Korean War gave the Shanghai municipal government leeway to try a more moderate approach, encouraging Legion of Mary members to register with the authorities and leave the organization in exchange for leniency. In an effort to revive the stalled Catholic Reform Movement, overtures were made to Chinese priests in Shanghai, including Gong Pinmei. Political pressure was kept up through the "patriotic" Catholic movement, but government support could not make up for this faction's lack of legitimacy. While one arm of the Party-state sought a negotiated solution, the public security organs prepared for future confrontations.[11] In a May 1954 speech to Public Security Bureau cadres, Luo Ruiqing, the national minister for public security, singled out Shanghai and its surrounding villages as "the deepest nest of imperialism based in China," but also admitted that the Public Security Bureau actually knew very little about the situation within the Catholic Church and had witnessed no evidence of "espionage" (although Luo attributed this to a lack of information rather than a true lack of counter-revolutionary activity).[12]

For the moment, instructions from the Party center were to oppose the activities of counter-revolutionaries within the Church while striving to win over the masses of believers to the anti-imperialist reform movement. This approach is reflected in a fascinating document from May 1954 about the problem of Catholic pilgrimages. That year had been declared by Pope Pius XII to be a Marian year (the first in the history of the Church). This declaration had an especially important resonance in China, where Marian devotion was strong as a result of both long-term trends (the Virgin Mary had been a popular figure among Jiangnan Catholics and especially women, perhaps because she bore a resemblance to Guanyin) and more recent causes (Marian devotion was a very important element of Catholic religiosity in the late nineteenth and early twentieth centuries, in particular the Marian apparitions Our Lady of Lourdes and Our Lady of Fatima, which was the time when missionary proselytization peaked in China). There are several Marian shrines in China that play a large role in the religiosity of Chinese Catholics, one of the most important being Our Lady of Sheshan 佘山, which has been a site of Catholic pilgrimages since the mid-to-late nineteenth century. The Marian Year was an occasion for the beleaguered Catholics of China to conduct pilgrimages to these shrines and fortify their faith. The CCP was concerned that the pilgrimages to Sheshan, such as one including hundreds of parishioners from Zhujiajiao 朱家角, in Qingpu district, would be an occasion for "spreading rumors [about the CCP's repression of Catholicism] everywhere." At the same time, the CCP was eager not to antagonize Catholics further and wanted to reiterate that they enjoyed freedom of religion so long as they split with counter-revolutionaries within the Church. The Party center therefore not only insisted that the pilgrimages be allowed to continue uninhibited but also tried to use them as an opportunity to promote the "progressive" clergy (进步神甫) who had joined or were amenable to the Reform Movement.[13]

CONFRONTATION

In 1955, the political mood in China took a decisive turn leftward in what came to be known as the "Socialist High Tide." In the political sphere, this was accompanied by a renewed campaign against intellectuals, especially the "Hu Feng counter-revolutionary clique" supposedly based in Shanghai, and a broad and intense campaign to "wipe out hidden counter-revolutionaries" (肃清暗藏的反革命分子). High on the list of targets was the Bishop of Shanghai, Ignatius Gong Pinmei. Having learned from the mistakes of the previous 4 years, units of the Public Security Bureau in Shanghai, working in concert with the Religious Affairs Bureau and other bureaucracies, methodically prepared a final assault on the intransigents within the Church. Over 1,000 cadres were assigned to plan a thoroughgoing propaganda campaign, struggle sessions, and eventually police raids against the Church in Shanghai. The hammer fell on September 8, 1955, with the arrest of Gong and some 300 members of his "counter-revolutionary clique," mostly intransigent militant Catholic youth and Chinese priests and seminarians seen as loyal to Gong. The media, in Shanghai and nationally, was ablaze with denunciations of Gong and his associates, and 2 weeks later, a massive public meeting was held, with some 10,400 Catholics in attendance, to denounce Gong. While Gong and his "clique" were whisked off to prison, where some of them would remain for decades, a citywide Catholic Patriotic Committee 上海天主教友爱国委员会 was established and, in the following months, Shanghainese Catholics were subjected to continuous, tiresome political "education" meetings to expound upon the seriousness of Gong's crimes.[14]

The Catholic opponents of the regime's heavy-handed religious policies had suffered a serious setback in 1955, but the political opening-up of the Hundred Flowers campaign the following year demonstrated plainly that the CCP had failed to "win over the masses" of Catholics in Jiangnan. Party cadres were shocked at the wellspring of civic activity that had seemingly disappeared in the preceding years but was in fact only lying dormant. When Catholics in Jiangsu were encouraged to express their views, they voiced sympathy for their arrested coreligionists and complained that the repeated campaigns against counter-revolutionaries felt like campaigns to eradicate religion. Patriotic Catholic activists were on the defensive, in some cases having to defend themselves from the "arrogant" attacks of those who had been arrested and recently released. Clergy and laity alike were weary of endless political campaigns and repetitive propaganda. Throughout Jiangsu, Catholics advocated the autonomous management of Church affairs and a new "constructive phase" of religious activity to replace the "destructive phase" of past struggle. Clerics also asked the government to sign contracts for compensation to make up for the foreign funds cut off in 1950, stating that "without economic freedom, religious freedom is not guaranteed." Above all, Catholics expressed concerns about the future, fearing that the move toward socialism and the conflict between "materialism" and "idealism" would result in religious repression, which is in fact exactly what happened during the "High Maoist" period of 1958–1976.[15]

A report on rural areas of Jiangsu claimed that Public Security Bureau and militia units were shot through with adherents to the "three religions and nine schools" (三教九流, referring to Buddhism, Daoism, Confucianism, and folk religion). In some villages, it was discovered that improperly vetted cadres and New Democratic Youth League members had in fact come from Catholic families and continued to help Catholic members of their community by writing them letters of introduction. In one case, a non-Catholic party cadre had stopped paying his party dues and converted to Catholicism. There had also apparently been a religious revival in the Catholic villages of Jiangsu: Songjiang, Fengxian, and Donghai counties, each of which had seemingly less than a thousand Catholics in 1956, suddenly counted several thousand Catholics.[16] Cadres of the Public Security Bureau and Religious Affairs Bureau tasked with monitoring these issues were at a loss as to how to react; under the aegis of the Hundred Flowers and freedom of religion, the "pressure tactics" of the past were not permissible, and priests were left to openly proselytize.

In Shanghai as well, the Hundred Flowers led to open expressions of displeasure over recent events. As a sign of good will, the city government invited prominent "moderate" Catholic laity, including Zhu Kongjia, Gu Shouxi 顾守熙, and Dong Guimin 董贵民, to join the Shanghai People's Congress and People's Political Consultative Committee. Sensing that it was safe to speak freely, Zhu publicly advocated the release of Gong Pinmei, whom he considered misguided rather than a traitor, to improve Catholic unity, and questioned the designation of the Legion of Mary as reactionary, claiming that if having some reactionary members made an entire organization reactionary, then the CCP itself could also be labeled as such. Other prominent Catholics called for reestablishing economic and political relations with the Vatican, allowing the Church to accept foreign funding and permitting the Church to operate independent religious schools and issue publications free from political oversight. Some even suggested returning property and institutions that had been made public or "jointly run" to the management of the Church. These demands seem naïve in retrospect, but they demonstrate the remarkable if brief openness of the Hundred Flowers period, as well as the latent dissatisfaction among Catholics, even those who were willing to work with the government.

For their efforts at negotiating between the two wings of the Catholic community, Zhu Kongjia and other moderate Catholics were swept up as "leading rightists" when the crackdown came in the summer of 1957. Accused of seeking to organize a "counter-revolutionary clique" to revive Gong Pinmei, they were repeatedly denounced as "poisoned arrows aimed at the CCP" in the national and local press. Along with Zhu and other Catholic lay leaders, leading clergy members in Shanghai and elsewhere who had shown reluctance in the past to "cut ties with imperialism" and denounce the Vatican were also condemned as rightists. It is no coincidence that the purge of Catholic "rightists" occurred at the time of the establishment of the CCPA and the definitive break with the Holy See.[17] The campaign against rightists provided the necessary cover for singling out recalcitrant priests who were defenseless after having so recently voiced deep criticisms of the party's policies.[18] On June 17, 1957, over 100 patriotic Catholic representatives from throughout China convened in Beijing to discuss the twin objectives of eliminating rightist influence in the Church and determining the future of Chinese Catholicism's relationship with the Vatican. On August 2, the conference wrapped up and the CCPA was established, defying threats of excommunication from Rome and setting Chinese Catholicism on a unique, semi-schismatic path down to the present.[19]

Meanwhile, throughout August and for several months afterward in 1957, the local and national press continued to trumpet the importance of eliminating imperialist influence in the Church. Echoing the Maoist rhetoric of the period, the Church's situation was regularly presented as a choice between two "lines" or "roads," one a patriotic embrace of socialism and the other a rightist resignation to the control of reactionaries and imperialism. In providing guidance on carrying out the latest effort to reform the Catholic Church, the Central Committee of the CCP instructed provincial and local party committees to enact policies according to local conditions, but otherwise to make no distinction between Catholic rightists and other rightists. Those who had been arrested in the past for counter-revolutionary activities and released were to be re-arrested and re-sentenced.[20]

Still, even after the political tide had clearly turned toward the suppression of "rightists," many Shanghainese Catholics exhibited "great contradictions." Throughout the Anti-Rightist Campaign and for months afterward, hundreds of Catholic youth and religious workers were forced to take part in "study sessions" and meetings to promote the "patriotic Church."[21] Rank-and-file Catholics were also subject to similar propaganda meetings as part of a wider "Socialist Education Movement."[22] Many remained defiant, daring cadres to throw them in prison for not attending study meetings. At the same time, big character posters were pasted on the walls of churches demanding the release of Gong Pinmei. The apparent "clean break" with the Vatican, in effect a schism, was greatly displeasing to rank-and-file Catholics and clergy alike. Even those Chinese priests whom the CCP hoped would lead the patriotic Church,[23] such as the Xujiahui parish priest Cai Zhongxian 蔡忠贤, cautioned that Catholics could not accept anything resembling a schism with Rome and would not support Zhang Shiliang, the elderly diocesan priest who nominally became acting bishop when Gong was arrested, or anyone else as bishop without Papal approval. Following the establishment of the CCPA, Religious Affairs Bureau cadres fretted that church attendance had plummeted, while the Jesuits continued to exhibit an uncooperative and "very arrogant attitude."[24]

By August 1958, a year of intense political struggle had led to the "autonomous" selection of more than a dozen bishops throughout China who rejected the "imperialist" control of the Vatican. A report sent by the United Front Work Department to the Central Committee of the CCP claimed victory for the patriotic Church; but it was a hollow victory indeed: most of China's 140 ecclesiastical jurisdictions had no bishop, Catholics were withdrawing from public religious life, and there were remnant Vatican loyalists everywhere in the Catholic community. Nonetheless, given the political climate of the "transition to socialism," there was no choice but to push forward. The Great Leap Forward signaled an intensification of all struggle and the party's rhetoric toward religion likewise intensified, attacking "superstition" and encouraging "materialism." In November 1958, religious activity ceased completely in stalwart Catholic communities in Songjiang, Jinshan, Fengxian, Nanhui, Qingpu, Chuansha, Chongming, and other counties in the countryside around Shanghai; churches were only reopened the following March,[25,26] once the Party was more certain of its grip on these churches' leadership. Although the CCPA had been established at a national level, the inability to win over a critical mass of lay and clerical supporters meant that it was not established in Shanghai until May 1960, at the height of the Great Leap Forward and soon after Gong Pinmei had been put on trial and sentenced to life in prison. Following Gong's sentencing, Zhang Jiashu 张家树 was named Bishop of Shanghai without Vatican approval.[27]

Conclusion

The period from the end of the Second Sino-Japanese War to the start of the Great Leap Forward in 1958 saw the Catholic Church in China go through some of the most dramatic changes in its entire history. The war against Japan had badly damaged the Church's finances, although relief work performed during the war improved the image of the Church in the eyes of non-Christian Chinese. Furthermore, Chinese Catholics attained a national hierarchy in 1946, full diplomatic relations with the Holy See (which were later transferred to Taiwan with the Republic of China's government), and a whole host of new initiatives to centralize and improve all aspects of Church activities, most notably in the Catholic Central Bureau. Although the foreign concessions had been eliminated and the question of Church–state relations had not been entirely settled, the Nationalists were generally well-disposed toward Catholics, especially now that the Church had severed its ties with foreign powers. Catholics therefore had every reason to be hopeful that the postwar period would lead to a florescence of religious and charitable activities.

However, the hope of the postwar period was short-lived. Soon after fighting with the Japanese ended, the Church was under threat in northern China from the Communists, a group that foreign missionaries, at least, considered to be far worse than the Japanese. The Communists were eager to eliminate the last vestiges of foreign imperialism in China, including the missionaries who still held many leadership positions in the nominally indigenous Church, and to inculcate a Marxist worldview fundamentally at odds with the "idealism" of Catholicism. More immediately, the Communists' affinity for land reform threatened to erode the most fundamental financial base of the Church throughout the country. In conquering southern China, however, the Communists pursued much more moderate United Front policies, which led to a similar relationship between Church and state to that under the Nationalists. It was only with China's entry into the Korean War that a full-scale campaign against the Catholic Church began. However, the CCP's hope to promote an anti-imperialist, patriotic reform movement within the Catholic Church was a complete failure in Shanghai (and elsewhere); the intense political campaigns of 1951 and early 1952 only served to further convince "militant" Catholics that the CCP was intent on destroying religion. The CCP had scored some important victories, taking over most Catholic educational and charitable institutions, expelling most foreign missionaries, and developing bureaucracies to deal with religion, schools, and health (including cadres and activists planted in Catholic institutions), but internal party documents show that the Party was uncertain in its apparent control over Shanghai's Catholic community.

Following the Korean War, Church–state relations took a relatively moderate turn until the CCP's religious policy was caught up in the Socialist High Tide of 1955, when the "Gong Pinmei counter-revolutionary clique" became one of the high-profile targets in a campaign to eliminate hidden counter-revolutionaries. Even after the arrest of Gong and other militant Catholics,[28] the party still approached Jiangnan Catholics apprehensively, and the failure to win adherents to the patriotic Church became shockingly apparent with the Hundred Flowers campaign. Those who spoke up or sought to reassert Catholic rights in 1956 were swept away in the Anti-Rightist Campaign of 1957, creating a "legacy of counter-revolution" in which lay and clerical Catholic workers at the now state-affiliated churches, and state-managed charitable and religious organizations, continued to be monitored for their political attitudes by cadres and "activist" colleagues well into the 1960s. The Anti-Rightist Campaign and the Great Leap Forward greatly intensified the pace of the "transition to socialism," including the goal of minimizing if not eliminating religion. The establishment of the CCPA in 1957, only realized in Shanghai after intense political pressure in 1960, initiated a period of religious suppression that would peak with the closure and destruction of churches at the start of the Cultural Revolution and continue until the late 1970s.

NOTES

1. This campaign, its context, and its effects are covered in more detail in Paul Mariani, *Church Militant: Bishop Kung and Catholic Resistance in Communist Shanghai* (Harvard University Press, 2011).

2. Shanghai Municipal Archives (hereafter SMA) A72-2-395, "Longhua qu dianxun xiang zenyang guanche dang de zhengce fadong tianzhujiao tu kaizhan hezuohua yundong" 龙华区电讯乡怎样贯彻党的政策发动天主教徒开展合作化运动.

3. SMA A71-2-180-27, "Zhonggong Shanghai shi Longhua qu weiyuanhui guanyu qibao tianzhujiao tu baowei zhen zhengfu qingkuang de baogao" 中共上海市龙华区委员会关于七宝天主教徒包围镇政府情况的报告. Villagers would not necessarily have been well disposed toward the Guomindang; when trying to prevent the Communist advance in May 1949, Nationalist troops intentionally blew up the bell tower and spires of the church in Qibao because they were obstructing an artillery unit's line of fire. After being arrested in 1955, Gong and Fu were accused of distributing anti-Communist propaganda and forcing parishioners to sing counter-revolutionary songs in Qibao; "Shanghai shi aiguo tianzhujiao tu fenfen kongsu he jielu Gong Pinmei fangeming jituan de zuixing" 上海市爱国天主教徒纷纷控诉和揭露龚品梅反革命集团的罪行, *Renmin ribao* 人民日报, December 11, 1955.

4. In the early 1950s, Fu was placed in charge of finances for the diocese, which is to say that he filled the role of procurator. However, Jin Luxian claimed that the French Jesuits Lacretelle and Germain continued to hold influence over Ignatius Gong Pinmei and therefore over the Church's finances. In any event, Fu was arrested with Gong in September 1955 and spent the next twenty-five years in labor camps and prisons; after being released in the early 1980s, he was re-arrested and sentenced to fifteen years imprisonment but then released in 1988; Jin Luxian, *The Memoirs of Jin Luxian*, ol. 1, p. 157.

5. "政府有群众, 我们也有群众, 看谁的力量大!".

6. Xia Genfu 夏根福, ed., Wang Xiaojian comp.; 王孝俭总纂; 上海市闵行区七宝镇人民政府编, *Qibao zhenzhi* 七宝镇志 (Shanghai: Shanghai renmin chubanshe, 2010), Chapter 27; "Zhonggong Shanghai shi Longhua qu weiyuanhui guanyu qibao tianzhujiao tu baowei zhen zhengfu qingkuang de baogao".

7. *Qibao zhenzhi*, p. 200.

8. *Qibao zhenzhi*, p. 495.

9. "Zai zongjiao waiyi de yangai xia—Gong Pinmei fangeming jiyuan zuixing zhi er" 在宗教外衣的掩盖下——龚品梅反革命集团

罪行之二, *Renmin ribao*, December 11, 1955. See also, "Weishanzhe de zhen mianmu" 伪善者的真面目, *Jiefang ribao* 解放日报, September 14, 1955.

10. "Longhua qu dianxun xiang zenyang guanche dang de zhengce fadong tianzhujiao tu kaizhan hezuohua yundong." The photocopies of deeds were later used as evidence against Gong in his 1960 show trial; Mariani, *Church Militant*, p. 192. The politics of the Eucharist have been common in Chinese Catholic Churches since the 1950s and recall the symbolic importance of the Eucharist for Catholics in previous religious struggles, such as the Wars of Religion in early modern Europe.

11. This was common practice with people seen as politically unreliable (former Guomindang officials and soldiers, landlords and their family members, etc.) even if they had not engaged in obviously counter-revolutionary activity; Mariani, *Church Militant*, pp. 75–99, 106–108.

12. Song Yongyi, ed., *Database of Chinese Political Campaigns in the 1950s: From Land Reform to State-Private Joint Ownership (1949–1956)* (hereafter DCPC), "Luo Ruiqing zai diliuci quanguo gongan huiyi shang guanyu 'Jin yibu jiaqiang renmin gongan gongzuo wei baozhang guojia shehuizhuyi jianshe he shehuizhuyi gaizao de shunli shishi er douzheng' de baogao" 罗瑞卿在第六次全国公安会议上关于"进一步加强人民公安工作为保障国家社会主义建设和社会主义改造的顺利实施而斗争"的报告, May 17, 1954.

13. DCPC, "Zhongyang fudui tianzhujiao shengmu nian jiti chaosheng huodong de chuli wenti" 中央复对天主教圣母年集体朝圣活动的处理问题, May 1, 1954.

14. Mariani, *Church Militant*, Chapter 4. See also SMA A22-1-233, "[Shanghai Zhonggong xuanchuan weiyuanhui] guanyu Shanghai tianzhujiao gongzuo de jieshao" [上海中共宣传委员会]关于上海天主教工作的介绍.

15. "Jiangsu sheng zongjiao jie sixiang dongxiang" 江苏省宗教界思想动向, *Neibu cankao* 内部参考, May 21, 1957.

16. *Neibu cankao*, May 14, 1957.

17. "Shanghai tianzhujiao shengceng youpai fenzi de dongxiang" 上海天主教上层右派分子的动向, *Neibu cankao*, June 28, 1957; "Aiguo de tianzhujiao tu fanji neibu youpai fenzi, buxu fan digang jiaoting ganshe woguo neizheng" 爱国的天主教徒反击内部右派

分子，不许梵蒂冈教廷干涉我国内政, *Renmin ribao,* September 31, 1957. Also mentioned in Jin Luxian, *The Memoirs of Jin Luxian,* Vol. 1, pp. 163, 174, 217. In Jin's telling, this group of moderate Catholic lay leaders had been convinced, like most Catholics in Shanghai, not to support the Three-Self Movement by Gong Pinmei.

18. As had been the case since 1949, campaigns against the Catholic Church occurred within the framework of wider crackdowns, or "leftist deviations.".

19. On perhaps the trickiest issue of all, that of electing bishops, a decision was made to appoint them independently but to inform the Vatican after the fact. This represented a reluctant concession to the clergy, as even patriotic Catholic clergy did not seek a schism and hoped to maintain some connection with the Vatican on this question. The United Front Work Department, on the other hand, presented this as a measure that would hopefully disappear with time as the Chinese Church became fully independent. See "Shenru kaizhan tianzhujiao fandi aiguo yundong" 深入开展天主教反帝爱国运动, *Renmin ribao,* August 3, 1957. It is worth noting that although a number of priests in Shanghai, including Zhang Shiliang, had sided with the patriotic Catholics, the most prominent public faces of Shanghainese patriotic Catholicism were laymen in Hu Wenyao and Yang Shida (another prominent local lay supporter of the CCPA was Lu Weidu 陆微读, the son of Lu Bohong). In January 1962, a second national meeting of the National CCPA was held in Beijing, where Yang and Zhang Jiashu, who replaced Gong as Bishop, were named vice-chairmen of the organization.

20. "Shanghai tianzhujiao you yi shiji xingdong xuanshi aiguo juexin, daliang jiefa jiao nei youpai jituan zuixing, xie xin gei rendaihui biaoshi yiding yao zou shehuizhuyi daolu" 上海天主教友以实际行动宣示爱国决心, 大量揭发教内右派集团罪行, 写信给人代会表示一定要走社会主义道路, and "Zhu Kongjia youpai xiao jituan yinmou bailu, zai daliang shishi mianqian chengren goujie diguozhuyi he baobi fangeming" 朱孔嘉右派小集团阴谋败露, 在大量事实面前承认勾结帝国主义和包庇反革命, *Wenhuibao* 文汇报, August 17, 1957. The party center advised the Religious Affairs Bureau to respect patriotic Catholics, develop "progressive forces" within the Church, and "win over and unite the middle

elements to push forward the struggle against imperialism and capitalism." In this struggle, "defections" from the CCPA were seen as "not such a terrible thing," as they would unmask the rightists and differentiate them from "the majority of believers"; DCPC, "Zhonggong zhongyang pifa zongjiao shiwu ju dangzu guanyu Zhongguo tianzhujiao daibiao huiyi de baogao" 中共中央批发宗教事务局党组关于中国天主教代表会议的报告, December 10, 1957.

21. During one such meeting, priests were gathered to discuss Mao's statements on imperialism and reactionaries being "paper tigers" and the "East wind prevailing over the West wind." Rather than parrot the slogans of the materials they were given, the priests noted the dangers of either China or the Soviet Union engaging in an armed conflict with the U.S. and questioned how quickly China could close the development gap with Western countries (the context of the Great Leap Forward is important to note); "Shanghai shi tianzhujiao shenfu dui dongfeng yadao xifeng wenti de fandong yanlun" 上海市天主教神甫对东风压倒西风问题的反动言论, *Neibu cankao*, December 6, 1958.

22. Mariani, *Church Militant*, 185. Not to be confused with the Socialist Education Movement, also called the Four Clean-Ups, which began in 1963 following the Great Leap Forward and the subsequent great famine. The 1960s Socialist Education Movement is increasingly being investigated by historians as more sources become available; preliminary information suggests that, among other targets, this movement sought to minimize if not eliminate religious activity itself (beyond just "counter-revolutionary" individuals or groups), and therefore led quite naturally into the anti-religious suppression of the Cultural Revolution era. On Catholicism during the Four Clean-ups, see Harrison, *The Missionary's Curse*, Chapter 6.

23. Shanghai Tongzhi Compilation Committee, ed., *Shanghai Tongzhi Vol. 14 "Ethnicity, Religion," Chapter 5 "Catholicism," Sect. 1*上海通志 > > 第十四卷民族、宗教 > > 第五章天主教 > > 第一节 沿革(http://www.shtong.gov.cn/node2/node2247/node79044/node79328/node79344/userobject1ai103698.html).

24. *Neibu cankao*, August 14, 1957. In the meantime, James Walsh, the former head of the Catholic Central Bureau, had remained as the last foreign missionary in Shanghai and was allowed relative

freedom of movement until he was arrested in 1958. The reasons for this are unclear, but there are four possible explanations, all of which proceed from the CCP's genuine belief that Walsh was more useful as a free man than he was in prison or expelled. The first explanation is that they genuinely believed him to be at the center of a spy ring throughout China and hoped they could collect further information by allowing him to move about and correspond relatively freely. Walsh's mail and other communication were monitored and pro-government "moles" were placed in his office. The second possible explanation is that he was kept around as a potential means of communicating with the Vatican and perhaps the U.S. government. Although he was virtually powerless after the closure of the CCB, Walsh received mail in Shanghai from Propaganda Fide in Rome that, in cryptic terms, seemed to suggest the possibility of an agreement with Chinese government. Walsh may have also been kept around as a "showpiece" to demonstrate to foreign visitors coming through Shanghai that there was freedom of religion in China. Finally, Walsh's continued, albeit isolated (Walsh spoke Cantonese but not Mandarin or Shanghainese), presence in Shanghai may have been maintained to confuse Shanghainese Catholics about how to approach "schismatic" priests. In any event, Walsh was finally arrested in 1958, put on trial at the same time as Gong Pinmei in 1960, and imprisoned for the next decade. Walsh's release in 1970 was one of the earliest steps of the Sino-American détente that would bring President Nixon to Shanghai two years later. Maryknoll Mission Archives, Bishop James E. Walsh Papers Series 5, Box 6, undated letter from winter 1955–1956 (probably January); Raymond Kerrison, *Bishop Walsh of Maryknoll: Prisoner of Red China* (G.P. Putnam's Sons, 1962), p. 307.

25. DCPC, "Zhongyang pizhuan guowuyuan zongjiao shiwu ju dangzhu guanyu tianzhujiao zixuan zisheng zhujiao gongzuo zhong de jige juti wenti he yijian de baogao" 中央批转国务院宗教事务局党组关于天主教自选自圣主教工作中的几个具体问题和意见的报告, July 30, 1958.

26. A report by the Beijing Committee of the Communist Youth League (formerly the New Democratic Youth League), forwarded throughout the country, discussed how to counter the influence of religion when working with Catholic classmates. While

patience and persuasion were emphasized, there was no question that there were "profound contradictions" between socialism and religion, and that a "serious political-ideological struggle" was needed to inculcate materialism and scientific thinking and replace religious superstition; DCPC, "Gongqingtuan zhongyang zhuanfa gongqingtuan Beijing shiwei 'Guanyu tianzhujiao dui shaonian de zongjiao mixin yingxiang de zhongdian diaocha he gongzuo yijian de baogao'" 共青团中央转发共青团北京市委"关于天主教对少年的宗教迷信影响的重点调查和工作意见的报告, December 4, 1959.

27. The CCP had held Gong in limbo for nearly five years in the hope that he could be convinced to lead the independent patriotic Church in Shanghai. Gong refused and spent most of the next thirty years in prison, being secretly elevated to Cardinal by Pope John Paul II in 1979. After months of ideological preparations, when it came time to sentence Gong and his co-conspirators, including Jin Luxian, the verdict of course was not in doubt. All that was left was to gauge the reaction to the verdict among the Catholic community. The leaders of the patriotic camp, no doubt feeling emboldened, played their part with special zeal. Some in the "leftist" camp even expressed displeasure that Gong had not been sentenced to death for his activities in the service of American imperialism. Those opposed to the proceeding expressed their displeasure in various ways. One priest slept through most of the hearing and several refused to participate in the "face-to-face" denunciations of Gong. Rank-and-file Catholics who had been enlisted to attend the hearing to grant it greater legitimacy contrived excuses to stay away. When Catholics were corralled into a mass meeting at Xujiahui just after the verdict was issued, a group of nuns were audibly distressed by the events of the day. "Shanghai shi zongjiao jie renshi dui shenpan Gong Pinmei anjian de fanying" 上海市宗教界人士对审判龚品梅案件的反应, *Neibu cankao*, March 22, 1960.

28. SMA A71-2-1977, Zhonggong Shanghai shiwei xuanchuanbu/Zhonggong Shanghai shi jiaogongwei xuanchuanbu 中共上海市委宣传部/中共上海市郊工委宣传部, "Guanyu daji he quchu tianzhujiao nie diguo zhuyi fenzi douzheng de xuanchuan tigang (xiuzheng gao)" 关于打击和驱除天主教内帝国主义分子斗争的宣传提纲 (修正稿), June 20, 1953; "Shanghai jiaotong daxue

deng wu xiao jiaoshi dui yuan xi tiaozheng de fanying" 上海交通大学等五校教师对院系调整的反映, *Neibu cankao*, August 22, 1952.

CHAPTER 7

A Letter From an Ex-Altar Boy to Late Fathers

Sheng-mei Ma

Abstract This autobiographical piece narrates how I as a young boy stumbled into Catholicism because the church near my *juancun*, Victory New Village, was the only venue where I could meet girls in a gender-segregated educational system in the 1960s Taiwan. Juancun, literally "military dependents' villages," were the housing complexes across Taiwan hastily slapped together in the wake of the Nationalist retreat from China in 1949 to accommodate the flood of military personnel and their families. I first laid out a map of Victory New Village, the mandala for this ex-altar boy. I met Father Hou Guizi from Hebei, China, and Father Marcel Legault, SJ, from Montreal, Canada. This is an ex-alter boy's fading memories of two Fathers and the Father in Heaven.

S. Ma (✉)
Michigan State University, East Lansing, MI, USA
e-mail: mash@msu.edu

C. Y. Chu (ed.), *The Catholic Church, The Bible, and Evangelization in China*, Christianity in Modern China,
https://doi.org/10.1007/978-981-16-6182-2_7

129

Keywords Taiwan's *Juancun* · Victory new village · Altar Boy · Father Hou Guizi · Father Marcel Legault

As a young boy, I stumbled into Catholicism because the church near my *juancun* (military dependents' village), Victory New Village, was the only venue where I could meet girls in the gender-segregated educational system of 1960s Taiwan. Juancun were housing complexes hastily slapped together across Taiwan in the wake of the Nationalist retreat from China in 1949 to accommodate the flood of military personnel and their families. If memory serves, Victory New Village in Taipei was first laid out as a rectangular grid from south to north, but it secreted a horizontal pyramid lying sideways from west to east, from Section Ding (D) to Section Jia (A). Possibly four vertical through streets divided each east–west block into housing project–style row houses, which became incrementally bigger from Sections D to A. I suspect that it was four rather than three through streets because Section D, with the smallest units, was further divided into two segments. Looking back, it dawns on me that the rectangular village was a mirage over the horizontal pyramid, with multiple units at the base on the west side to hold up the superstructure of a few mansions on the east side: a beehive supporting the queen bee, so to speak. A miniature Manhattan mapped by parallel streets and perpendicular avenues, Victory New Village's evenly divided grids of blocks and streets shrouded chasmic socioeconomic divides. The swarms of mainland transplants across Taiwan appeared identical, though; even the name Victory New Village was assigned to duplicate communities in various cities. Visualize my village as a scroll of Chinese calligraphy authored by the Nationalist government, starting from the northeastern corner with thick ink and fresh vigor through the first few vertical lines, but getting faster and sloppier toward the end at the southwestern corner.

My tenement home was number 245 of Block 2, Section D, sitting at the bottom, whereas those single-family homes in Section A in the east end flaunted their red brick walls that were so high that passersby were not able to peep into the yard and the house inside. I could not tell exactly how big these houses were, nor whether there were variations within the seven blocks of Victory New Village. My activities took me mostly to the public playground on Block 4, where I caught big-headed black ants (*Camponotus friedae*—native to Taiwan, I believe) near the culvert and drowned them in my glass vials or tied strings to the "Heavenly Ox"—a wood-chewing brown beetle with two long, ribbed antennas—and let it fly in circles. My actions to ants and beetles and butterflies and grasshoppers and cicadas were so vile and cruel because I felt like an insect, squashed and looked down upon by those higher up. This binarism was fraught, though, for each segment contained considerably bigger corner units with a yard. I was too young and too self-conscious to measure the length and width for careful parsing decades later; neither could I do so later in my dreams, as vivid as they come each night. Thank you, dear reader, for your patience as I have laid out this map of Victory New Village, the mandala for this ex-altar boy, with the altar smack at the heart of number 245. From this mental maze, a flea fancied fleeing west, but first made a short hop to the Christian sacristy where it played dress-up in a surplice weekly (see Fig. 7.1).

The Sacred Heart Church of Our Lady lay in the southwestern corner at the end of Block 1, latching onto Victory New Village like an infant suckling. The small back door of the church, a red iron door standing on concrete poured over the village sewer, was the feeding mouth that also fed the community. I received catechism and was baptized there, serving as an altar boy every Sunday, donning the habit, swinging the incense burner, and shaking the bell during Mass for dramatic effect. During the impoverished days of the Cold War, children would queue up after Mass for handouts, one piece per person, delivered into the raised palm like a wafer: nutritious supplements donated by the US, such as chewable vitamin pills, biscuits, and other goodies that I no longer recall. Tall, kind, and inclined to mumble under his breath, Father Hou Guizi 侯桂滋 from Hebei, China, presided over the church. In my last visit to the church in 2013, I found an inscription in his honor carved into the marble slab at the foot of the newly renovated six-story church (Fig. 7.2).

In high school, I felt I had outgrown that small church and began to attend the Holy Family Cathedral quite far away, one of the largest in Taiwan, in part because there were more girls there. I did marry one on whom I first laid eyes on the front steps to the cathedral, and she became my better half. A Jesuit priest from Montreal, Canada, Father Marcel Legault 高道興, took charge of nearly all the youth organizations. I kept in touch with him over the years, even after I went overseas. I witnessed his decline due to Alzheimer's, when he was unable to locate his telephone on the desk sitting right in front of him. Perhaps he no longer recognized the shape of a telephone. Hearing about his bedridden

Fig. 7.1 The Altar Boy

last days howling in sheer agony and seeing that plaque at the foot of a
wall at a bustling street corner, I was struck by the indifference of the
Heavenly Father to His loyal servants' suffering, if He ever lived. Even if
He had, was He too senile to mind Father Legault, just as Father Legault

Fig. 7.2   Father Hou's memorial inscription

was too senile to find the telephone? Based on the scanty photographs from those austere days, when cameras and negatives were luxuries, this is an ex-altar boy's memory of the late Father Hou, Father Legault, and the Father, near and dear to that boy, so far away now—llike phone lines disconnected, dead. Fathers in heaven, forgive this transgression of an apostate!

Hardly an apostate if the motive were to meet my mate rather than my Maker. More broadly, I was driven by an urge to get out of my constricted life in a boxed-in, stifling juancun—to get as far away as possible. This outward trajectory culminated in a life's journey to the West for a career at an English Department in a university in the American Midwest, figuratively in the middle of the West. Catholicism, after all, came from the West. Serendipitously, both the Sacred Heart Church of Our Lady and the Holy Family Cathedral lay to the west of Victory New Village. The former was just a block away from me to the southwest, the latter further away, due west by bus. My family did get out of Victory New Village when we moved westward to Twin Creek district. All four brothers in my family, plus my parents, eventually relocated to the US, the fate of many mainlanders, or *waishengren* (foreign-province people) deemed outsiders by Taiwanese and oftentimes by themselves. Yet this ultimate journey to the West required, physically, bearing East, flying eastbound across the Pacific Ocean and the International Date Line, as if against the clock—turning back time in flight; night reversing itself into day.

Bearing East, however, is a double entendre, or perhaps even a triple and quadruple one. Wu Cheng'en's sixteenth-century classic *Journey to the West* imagines the Tang dynasty monk Tripitaka's expedition with three monstrous disciples to India to acquire Buddhist sutras. Having overcome the 81 calamities along the way, the monk returned to the capital Chang'an and, for the remainder of his life, settled down to translate the Sanskrit sutras, inaugurating sinologized Buddhism. "There and Back Again," as Bilbo Baggins entitles his memoirs, seems more fitting for Wu's Pilgrim's Progress. Journey to the West implies a journey back; bearing East means to turn to the east, precisely what I am doing now toward the end of my voyage. This turn of mine would bear or give birth to the past that is no more, other than in my mind. This bearing or siring East necessitates baring or searing the East to reopen old wounds, forgotten wonders, and everything in between. The East is yeast for my round trip, physically and psychologically, to the West and back.

Figure 7.3 captures Father Hou laying his hands on my shoulders as we stand outside the church hallway. Ever so gentle, the placement of Father Hou's fatherly hands, however, may have stemmed from the presence of the other father taking the picture—my father, who considered the camera his prized possession. The camera in my father's hands parallels the altar boy in Father Hou's. Rather than the Father, the Son, and the Holy Ghost, the picture intimates two Ghostly Fathers and one son, who stares back at the abyss. The plaque behind us over the arch of the hallway reads: "Ten Thousand Springs from One True Source." The pun on *yuan* (source, spring) suggests the Lord, from Whom all life originates, and by Whom, like spring water, all life is sustained. The rounded calligraphic script resembles those bestowed by the Qing emperor Kangxi to Beijing's Jesuit cathedral in the seventeenth century.

Looming over the picture were in effect four patriarchs: Father Hou in the picture, my father taking the picture, the Qing emperor who sanctioned the Jesuits, and the Heavenly Father. The quaternity was no accident. Jesuit priests following Marco Polo targeted the royal court

Fig. 7.3 Father Hou and the author at the Sacred Heart Church

as the pivot for missionary success. Like favored like, so the seat of Catholicism, the Vatican, reached out to the seat of Chinese power, the emperor, before Catholicism radiated to adjacent provinces such as

Father Hou's Hebei. Withdrawing with Chiang Kai-shek from Communist China to Taiwan, serviced primarily heretofore by Baptists and Presbyterians, including the renowned George Leslie Mackay of Canada, the Catholic Church found its footholds near ready ears of congregates of mainlanders. Victory New Village provided lifeblood to the Sacred Heart Church, just as the even larger Jiannan New Village and Luyue New Village across from the Holy Family Cathedral did. Jiannan and Luyue formed the site of the present-day Daan Forest Park.

In the distance, directly in front of me and Father Hou, was a very high slide built of concrete at the end of a long playground with swings, monkey bars, and other facilities on either side. The slide was the smoothest one that I recall from my childhood, due to its heavy use. Now that I look back at this setting, the children's playground was apparently not deserted all week long in anticipation of young weekend worshippers before and after (preferably not during) the Sunday Mass. Indeed, the church ran a kindergarten with a sizeable playground for the children. Why didn't I go there? Why did I attend Victory Kindergarten instead, further away at the east end of Block 4? Cost, rather than my family's faith, was probably the reason. The front gate to the church is out of frame to the right of Father Hou; two huge iron doors sliding out in grooves through which the kindergarten van drove to deliver kindergarteners. Given its proximity to Victory New Village and its large families, parents could have walked their kindergartners over within minutes. Why the bother to "bus" kindergartners in? The van most likely picked up children outside the Village, an alternative universe to my childhood.

The narrow staircase behind me and Father Hou led up to the nave, with the sacristy at the end of the aisle. That aisle was also the place where the "breadline" of children would form to collect their Sunday reward; I remember our keen disappointment when there were no sweets. The window right behind us was Teacher Yang's office, where I received my catechism. Teacher Yang and several other female teachers doubled as church youth counselors and kindergarten staff. During puberty, this boy from a family of four brothers sat week after week beside a young woman in a fashionable miniskirt of the day. One particular session is burned into my memory. As Teacher Yang elaborated on a religious story that I have totally forgotten, the young woman's skirt had scrunched so high up her thighs that (lo and behold!) I witnessed the thick spandex band holding her stockings in place. Having at the time never seen such female apparel,

I describe it with the wisdom of hindsight. At the time, I was so shocked by that strip that I felt she must have done it deliberately. A vision of heaven, pure ecstasy revealed by the Goddess to the Chosen!

Truth be told, though, that dark band of my crush has long dimmed with the passage of time; I even had difficulty recalling Teacher Yang's surname before I typed up this letter. Checking my birthday against those of the apostles, she decided that mine was closest to John's and hence gave me the baptismal name Ruowang (若望), the transliteration of John or Johann. She had no idea how right she was: on the surface, Ruowang meant looking forward to, awaiting (for instance, the coming of the Messiah) but the homophone of *wang* (望, to expect) is to forget (忘). To be named after the schizophrenic prophet of the Book of Revelation foreshadowed a life split between two continents and between two languages: remembering what had once been dis-membered; forgetting what had once been the apple of my eye, the forbidden fruit of knowing; communicating in English what had once been experienced in Chinese; sharing with the millennial, secular, and Anglophone public flashes of memory from half a century ago on the dark side of the world.

Figure 7.4 shows Father Legault, whom we nicknamed Lao Gao (Old Gao). This intimate nickname betrayed a certain amount of disrespect, as one would address an inferior employee, such as a janitor, as Lao plus his surname. Only among people of the same generation and similar status would Lao be acceptable. Suffice to say, Lao Gao was many decades senior to us in the youth groups, but in this context it demonstrated how close we felt toward him, as though he were one of us. I hereby translate the short letter, written in Chinese, that I slogged through on my computer's newly installed pinyin program in 2012 to contribute to a memorial volume after his passing.

Lao Gao,

I've always wanted to write your biography, but I've been overseas, so there was no way to start. Besides, when I returned occasionally over the years, I visited you at Fu Jen University in Taipei and you always dismissed it on account of your uneventful life that would be pointless to chronicle. Now it's too late.

As Sister Sun is compiling this memorial volume in your honor, I may as well send you a letter. If there are such things as souls, I imagine that you no longer suffer from old-age dementia and would understand my regret. If there is no soul, no God, all becomes in vain. This letter would be futile.

Fig. 7.4   Father Marcel Legault, SJ (1926–2012)

Still, futility leaves behind words, like traces of your life, imprinted in the thoughts of many.

You were plagued by Alzheimer's in the last years of your life. I visited you twice in Hsingchu during my visits to Taiwan for conferences. You remembered my name but you could not locate the telephone on your desk. I froze because it sat right in front of you. I asked you to sign your name card. No problem with Marcel Legault, S. J., done with a flourish. Yet you asked me how to write "Gao." Seeing your frantic embarrassment, I began to wonder if there were God. If there were, why was He so callous to his loyal servant? Perhaps He had gone too senile to remember all the Jesuit missionaries.

The flood of memory, all the way back to high school when I first met you at the Holy Family Cathedral. We shook hands and I felt your strong grip. Except for this, I knew nothing about you. Many years later, we had long and hearty conversations at your Fu Jen University office, which was in fact the university doorman's station at the front gate. We dined too, at the restaurant right outside of National Tsing Hua University. And in Hsingchu . . . All those images, the pang of recollection. As much as I wish to write, I can't seem to find the pinyin rendering of specific Chinese ideograms. The same story, enacted by different characters at different places: my memory, which the computer fails to piece together; your living quarters, where you failed to pinpoint the telephone; the boss in heaven has likewise forgotten the errand boy on earth. You said you had lived an ordinary life, one given to the relentless rush of chores, scraping together tea and beverages, moving chairs and desks for high schoolers and college students and the congregation and Jesuit brothers! Now that you're done with your show, has it been a tragicomedy, or a theater of the absurd? Has it been the Divine Comedy, or a hand puppet skit? Will you ever let me know?

The letter's ellipsis hides a moment much to my shame. As my family moved away from Victory New Village in the second year of my high school, I decided to quit the Holy Family Cathedral. Distance and the pressure of a college entrance exam two years later definitely played a role; but the mean streak in me, fueled by a sulk over not having had any steady relationship, turned me against Lao Gao. I took out my juvenile frustration and anger on him, much as I did on bugs. In his office up on the second floor of the cathedral, he was engaged in one of his endless "projects," soldering something. I told him that I would not attend the Sunday Mass ever again. "There was no point," I said over the buzz and smell of melting metal, "for there was no God." He went on soldering while tears began to well in his eyes. He never let them drop, though, because I remember my fear that the tears rolling around would crest. He finally laid down the soldering gun, giving his signature comic shrug while making a face of resignation. In a feigned light-hearted tone, he declared the project of joining two pieces of metal a lost cause, before turning, as I dreaded, to me, the other lost cause he was yet to give up. I have never ceased fleeing from those unfallen tears.

The allotted length is reached before I even get to the third and Heavenly Father; perhaps my allotted time on this earth will be up before I know Him. Just as well, I have neither a photograph nor mental image of Him on which to launch a thousand words. Yet to write this epistle at all, to let Him have a piece of my mind, and to share it widely, does it mean I still wish these late fathers were there holding my shoulders, holding the soldering gun, holding my hand as I turn toward what is to come?

INDEX

© The Editor(s) (if applicable) and The Author(s) 2022
C. Y. Chu (ed.), *The Catholic Church, The Bible, and Evangelization in China*, Christianity in Modern China,
https://doi.org/10.1007/978-981-16-6182-2

Lightning Source UK Ltd.
Milton Keynes UK
UKHW010640221222
414324UK00001B/228

9 789811 661846